MW01505557

TRANSFIGURATION
DIET

Why This Book?

In 1975, when our Think Tank's research began, we didn't set out to write a book. However, in our quest for health and longevity, our research yielded a radically different turnaround program for diet and health. Even though aspiring toward total health became a way of life for us, we hadn't realized that others might be interested in, or ready for, such a unique approach to nutrition and well-being. However, we were proven wrong. Others WERE interested--a lot of them.

The Transfiguration Diet is the result of eleven years of research. During that time our friends and those we worked with at our jobs began to notice what we were eating, how healthy and vibrant we looked, and how no one could keep up with our work pace.

Wherever we went--on planes, on trips, or to restaurants--many people said, "That sure smells good, what are you eating?" When we explained, they said, "How do I get started?" and "Where do I get a copy of your diet?" After we described the diet program and told them how much weight we lost or how some stopped having to take blood pressure medication, they responded, "Ok, that does it, I *have* to get started on this diet. This is what I've been waiting for."

Then people wanted further details. Our office phones began to ring, "What's the next step?" "What do I do now?" Letters of inquiry about our research increased, and we finally realized we weren't getting much done on our project.

We were delighted that people wanted to improve their health, but we didn't want those who had started on their own to get off the track because they had no book, no complete instructions, or anything to refer to. We knew for their sakes and ours that we needed to do something soon, especially when people kept asking, "When are you going to publish your diet? I want to know all of it."

So here are the results--the Transfiguration Diet--and what some people are saying about how it has helped them.

"A friend of mine whose brother is part of the Think Tank told me about this diet, and since being on it, I have lowered my blood pressure to the point that I no longer take blood pressure medicine 3 times a day. My blood pressure used to be 220/180 and now is 128/80. I don't think anyone could ask for more from a diet."
Lucky Pesao - Colorado Springs, CO

"I'm 5'10" and I used to weigh 220 pounds. After 5 months on your diet I'm down to 175 pounds. I eat as much as I want without constantly worrying about my weight because it stays where it should be. It's a load off my shoulders and a lot of other places too. I feel this is quite an accomplishment since several members of my family are considered obese."
Tom Welch - Albany, NY

"I had arthritis pains for years and moving around was very painful. Since being on the Transfiguration Diet my arthritis pains have completely disappeared. I can't believe it happened in just a few months. How can I get more detailed information? All I have is the basics."

Bett Deal - Albuquerque, NM

"I used to think I had a healthy body with plenty of vitality. When I heard about your Transfiguration Diet from a friend I just wanted to see if it would make me any healthier. I soon found out that my body did suffer from the improper diet of my past, and my lymphatic system was severely congested. I was on the road towards a battle with cancer. This diet triggered an immediate body cleanse, and I began to experience a rejuvenation and rebuilding of the unhealthy parts of my body."

Katia Frei - Vancouver, Canada

"I used to be skinny and pale. I'd eat and eat but could never gain a pound. Within a few months after starting on this diet I gained 15 pounds, was up to normal weight, and had some color in my cheeks. Everyone says I've never looked better. Thanks for putting up with all my phone calls. Let me know how I can help you in your efforts to get this information out to the public."

Chuck Mann - Cambridge, MA

"I've suffered from severe menstrual cramps for 20 years. I experienced chills, rises in body temperature, nausea, vomiting, diarrhea, along with extreme pain and cramping. Doctors prescribed hormones and birth control pills but nothing really helped. Then I was fortunate enough to hear about your work with the Transfiguration Diet and its herbal remedies. Since being on the diet I've not suffered any menstrual pain or symptoms. If anyone asks if I believe in miracles, I'd say 'Yes!' and your Think Tank sure gave me one to be thankful for."

Sarah Abel - Long Island, NY

"I have suffered from chronic constipation for over 25 years. Even though everyone always told me how healthy I looked, I knew my vitality was not what it could be. I can't say thank you enough, because for the first time my energy is so abundant and so even that life is really a joy. No colon resections for me."

Janice Reed, R.N. - Washington, D.C.

"I don't know what shape I'd be in if I hadn't run into one of your researchers on a plane and been given the basic ingredients for your diet--especially the part on genetics. I can't remember when I felt better. I used to suffer from cravings for food that led to eating almost anything I could get my hands on. After I had binged for several days, guilt and physical discomfort would take over and I'd be off on a fast trying to purge my system for the 'umpteenth' time. Now I have learned the key to controlling and reprogramming these genetic signals. Thank you. Thank you. Thank you."

Frederick Michaels - Ithaca, NY

"I was a die hard steak and eggs buff and never thought I could live without it. I thought meat was the only thing that gave me stamina, and was skeptical that this diet could sustain

me. I was proven wrong. I've been on the T.D. for several months without any of the sluggishness that usually followed my steak meals."

H.M. - Austin, TX

"I used to suffer from extreme stress which came out as irritability and impatience. I always blamed the pressure of my job, and never thought these could be a result of what I was eating. Since I've been on this diet, I have much more control of these areas. My friends have noticed the changes too."

Mr. Fred Mackey - San Diego, CA

"I have had strong recurring headaches ever since I was a teenager. I have followed the Transfiguration Diet and herbal remedies and feel that my chemistry and nutritional balance has been corrected. Now I can finally say, 'No more headaches!'"

Ann Fenton - Arlington,VA

"I used to be a chocoholic and craved sweets of all kinds. I'd skimp on meals so I could eat big, rich desserts. I loved that surge of energy, but I finally realized that these sugar 'highs' were quickly followed by energy lows and oftentimes irritability. I tried the Transfiguration Diet and found consistent vitality and less moodiness. And what's more, I can now walk by a bakery without batting an eye. Your Think Tank has done so much much for me, is there any way I can help you out?"

Denny Johnson - Eugene, OR

"My only wish is that I would have run into your diet sooner. Besides a weight problem, I had a hair trigger temper. After only several months, your diet quickly brought my weight to where it should be, but the biggest benefit is that I have ten times more control than before over sharp remarks and instant flare-ups. I had no idea that what I ate had such a profound effect on my disposition."

Mr. John Crain - Chicago, IL

"I didn't know that my diet had anything to do with my periodic spells of depression and anxiety. What I've learned in my correspondence with you has helped me understand how diet does play a significant role in my mental outlook. By eating the right foods it helps me maintain a more positive and happy attitude. It worked for me. Thank you."

Mr. Orange - New York, NY

"In the fall of 1984, I was diagnosed as having lost partial sight in my left eye due to glaucoma with a pressure reading of 39. In the following months there was an ever present fear of losing the sight completely. Prescribed medication could only lower the pressure to 30. Laser surgery brought the pressure down to 20 but this was still considered too high and required that additional medication be taken. I knew there must be something else I could do to save my eyesight. It was then that I heard about your Transfiguration Diet, something that could actually get to the cause rather than just the symptoms of the pressure build-up in my eye. After only a few months on your diet the pressure reading in my eyes is down to 13 (normal range). I'm convinced the Transfiguration Diet saved my sight. Thank you."

J. Nelson - Kansas City, MO

TRANSFIGURATION
DIET

An extraordinarily advanced "turn-around" concept regarding man and food—health OR disease!

Authored by an experienced health and nutrition research team who call themselves Littlegreen Inc.'s Think Tank.

Copyright ©1986 by Littlegreen , Inc.
Reprinted 1997 by Christopher Publications, Inc. with permissic

All rights reserved. No part of this book may be used or repro-
duced in any manner whatsoever without written permission,
except for brief quotations included in a review.

Printed in the United States of America.
Second Edition
ISBN 0-936863-04-8
Library of Congress Catalog Card Number 85-91090

The information and ideas in this book are not intended to be used as
guide for the diagnosis and/or treatment of any disease. Rather, this informati
is meant to help you work together with your physician in a mutual effort to
promote and maintain your health.

Anyone who uses this information without his doctor's approval is
prescribing for themselves and must assume the risks thereof. The author,
publisher, and distributors of this book are not responsible for any consequenc
resulting from the use of this diet or from an of the preparations or procedures
described in this book.

Any reference to brand names or trademarks in this book in no way
indicates that the companies involved endorse any findings or ideas that the
author is presenting.

Contents

one

The Big Decision

Overview

If you have finally awakened, as many others have, to recognize that it's high time you make drastic improvements in your eating habits, then this material is for you. And if you want the keys to making that change stick, this too is spelled out in a completely new approach.

You may be aware that only recently has the medical establishment begun to make the public aware of the link between obesity and genetic heritage. The truth is that not only obesity, but all eating habits, food cravings, and ways of thinking about eating are genetic.

Transfiguration Diet

These genetic characteristics regarding eating can be reprogrammed. In this book, we are not only presenting a diet that leads to a disease free, truly healthy body, we are also giving you the key to implement the diet with ease, by teaching you the way to reprogram your genes, and the way to be in control not only of your eating habits, but *every* aspect of your life.

We know that when we say "eating habits are genetic characteristics which can be reprogrammed," a natural tendency is to think, "Well, if eating habits are genetic, then I don't have any control over them, do I? I might as well accept the genetic package I have since I can't do anything about it." Nothing could be further from the truth. What we want to help you discover is that you *can* reprogram your genes. It is a very simple technique, although it does require a certain amount of effort and repetition. Once you begin the process, however, we think you'll be very proud to see the amazing accomplishments you can make. Your improved discipline, control, new eating habits, and advanced ways of thinking can't help but influence others around you. Others can't help but be curious and inspired to learn from your example, if they also are seeking improvement. Fortunately, this seems to be the beginning of a new social consciousness, and we all feel lucky to be a part of it.

Our research team, Littlegreen Inc.'s Think Tank, has spent 11 years studying nutrition, diet, health, genetic reprogramming, and other advanced ways of thinking. At times there are as many

as several dozen individuals working on a project. We come from varying occupations ranging from computer programmers and analysts to operating room nurses. We chose the name Littlegreen based on the public's use of "little green men" to symbolize more highly evolved, wise, and futuristic beings. We hoped this might stimulate interest in directing some individuals toward more *advanced* ways of caring for their overall health.

It is interesting to us that even though there have been a few books available for years on similar topics (mucusless diet, toxicless diet, raw food diets) and the information they contain is very important, they haven't caught on to any significant degree. Because of this, we felt a need to make a special effort to present a book with not only a meaningful content, but also in a format that is eyecatching and pleasant to read. Unfortunately, the public is often turned off by content oriented material which isn't wrapped in a "sparkling" cover, and we feel this information is too valuable to be lost on a shelf in a bookstore.

Our observation happily reveals that in many parts of the country people are finally waking up to appreciate the value of proper nutrition and the use of healthy foods, and we have no doubt that the time is ripe for this knowledge to come to the fore. We hope this little book will make a dent in turning around not only poor eating habits, but also the general abuse of the body that has been so prevalent in the last few decades. We hope that you, others, and even future generations can benefit by our sharing this knowledge and our experience with you.

True Health Explained

We know of nothing that has a greater influence on the degree of physical and mental health we experience, and our *longevity*, than the quality of food we put into our bodies and the quality of thoughts we entertain in our brains.

True health is not simply being free from acute or chronic disease. Just because we are not in a hospital bed, or confined to a wheelchair, or taking any medications, or missing days of work, does not mean we are healthy. We may have a body that feels and appears healthy now, but could this be a false or temporary image of health? Even though we might feel on top of the world today, we don't know what genetic weaknesses we might have to face down the line, and how we may be adding to the problem as a result of unhealthy eating habits. Why not get started working against any invisible genetic weaknesses? Why not give ourselves a better chance for preventing the development of disease?

Some people have such strong genetic characteristics that in spite of every abuse, they seem to reach a ripe old age. This certainly

shouldn't be a reason for others to challenge that this might be their case as well. It can take years of destructive eating habits before some diseases such as cancer, arthritis, or heart disease begin to show up. These conditions don't develop overnight. The fact that our bodies have a strong capability to compensate for the "junk foods" we put into them is no reason to take them for granted. If we continue to treat our bodies with little or no care and respect, we are inviting them to break down at an early age, and inviting latent genetic weaknesses to surface.

The frequency of colds, flu, bronchitis, asthma, menstrual difficulties, heart attacks, diabetes, skin disease, venereal disease, cysts, tumors, tiredness, lethargy, impatience, irritability, inability to concentrate, and stress are all signs of a civilization whose bodies are in a degenerative condition. This *can* be reversed. With the right foods, herbs, and improved habits and ways of thinking that result from genetic reprogramming, we can stop the degenerative process. We can then begin a cleansing, revitalizing, rebuilding process that will be the *beginning* of health and ultimately lead to extended life and productivity.

We know from our own experience what this Transfiguration Diet program has accomplished in giving us more vitality, evenness of temperament, higher perspectives in our thinking, and freedom from such common symptoms as headache, constipation, sluggishness, indigestion, and menstrual difficulties that accompany a traditional Western diet. We know these same benefits can now be yours.

Why "Transfiguration"

Transfiguration implies that by losing excess weight or gaining back needed weight, we transform our shape and appearance. More importantly, transfiguration means we can also be changed by the advanced concepts, attitudes, and ways of thinking that become a part of us as a result of genetic reprogramming. Thirdly, transfiguration refers to the chemical changes that result from the cleansing, healing, rebuilding qualities of the foods we consume which will alter the structure and function of every cell in our body.

Why bother with all this? Not only can we become more healthy, refined, controlled individuals, but we can alter the quality of genetic information we pass on to future generations as well. By replacing old established habits, old ways of thinking, and old genetic programming with new, more advanced concepts and understandings, we can rebuild our genes and rebuild the foundation for a new generation.

two

---

*Reprogramming
Your Genes
Re: Eating*

The Three I's--Who's Talking?

For the sake of understanding, it works best to picture or imagine that within each of us there are three I's, or three voices that use the word "I." For example, when we say, "I like so and so," if it's an intuitive like, or a like that's been with us most of our life instead of a disciplined like, it's the ancestral genetic heritage that is speaking (or the genes carrying that ancestral programming).

If it's a learned like that is not intuitive, it's probably the result of environmental influences or direct experiences we have had during this life that made a strong impression upon us. (The genes also house the environmental influences or experiences learned during this life.)

If we say, "I like such and such," and we like it only because we recognize the value of it, or feel it is more right even though we would intuitively tend to like the opposite, or if it is a disciplined like, then this is the mind talking and reflects a lesson learned in our genetic past. (Certain parts of our genetic structure also have pockets for housing the mind, what others refer to as spirit or soul.)

These three voices (mind-heritage-environment) all express themselves through the brain, so how do we learn to identify which voice is speaking? First, let's talk about our genetic heritage. A good analogy that works for us is to think of genes as tiny information chips, similar to those in a computer. They contain all the information passed on through our blood line (or ancestral heritage) regarding physical appearance and constitution; likes and dislikes; attitudes, responses, and ways of thinking; how we express ourselves; desires and opinions; weaknesses and strong points; literally everything about us. Subconsciously, these genes will respond automatically, transmitting those thoughts into our consciousness, and we interpret them simply as "our opinion" voicing itself.

We don't have to waste a lot of energy figuring out which source the voice is coming from. That investigation doesn't serve us, except in the understanding that the wise voice or mind, which has learned lessons, will be the source of responses that will choose to restrain us from destructive paths. Anything less than a response of restraint, because of a lesson learned, is the vehicle (body) talking--the voice of the genetic programming from the blood strain and/or environment.

It helps us to substitute the word "vehicle" for "body" in our vocabulary, because of the way most of us today are programmed to respond to these two words. In many cases, "body" is connected with lower (animal parallel) responses--manifesting in self-consciousness, modesty, and sensuality; whereas, "vehicle" is a more objective term not having those same associations.

The mind and vehicle are *completely separate*, the mind having existed before we ever came into this life. Again, the mind has no relationship to the genetic characteristics of the vehicle (neither to the genes programmed from the inherited blood line nor to those programmed by the environment during this life). Remember, we're not talking about the brain when using the word "mind." The brain is that part of the vehicle which acts as a receiver and transmitter of the genetic signals.

Our team's vernacular uses the word "mind" in the same context as religious terminology does in reference to the spirit or soul. The clarification of this usage is in no way intended to propose or endorse any particular religion, though the terminology could seem to suggest such. We're merely trying to clarify the understanding of this three-voice concept (mind-heritage-environment). Whether this terminology is suitable in the eyes of some is really of no concern to us. The fact is that using it to implement the concept of genetic reprogramming has proven unquestionably to work to a tee. The technique is so successful and yields such remarkable consistency in results that our team is currently involved in exploring this topic in depth.

The "I," in reference to the mind, speaks always with the most respectable and learned evaluation. For the sake of clarification, whenever we use the words I, we, or you, in this book, it is generally the mind we are referring to, that part of us which wants to improve. It is therefore "our" task (our mind's task) to talk to our vehicles, direct them in all their actions, and continually work to improve and refine the vehicle's genetic characteristics.

We're sure that most of you have employed this reprogramming technique anytime you exercised restraint or discipline for whatever motivational purpose. For example, if you avoided eating sweets because you wanted to lose weight, then you were unconsciously using this technique. In other

words, if a voice inside you says, "I really want a piece of candy," and you exercise discipline by coming back with "No, I'm *not* going to eat any," then this is an example of your mind talking back to your vehicle. Only the voice of the vehicle (the genetic programming) would state such a strong liking for a food you know is harmful, while the mind is the voice that tries to get you back on track.

Food as Fuel

We believe a more evolved concept of food is that it is simply *fuel* to supply the body with the nutrients and energy it needs. Putting fuel in a vehicle (body) can be treated as objectively as putting gasoline in an automobile. Even though most human vehicles are in the habit of eating for pleasure, and they associate having food with holidays, parties, celebrations, or family gatherings, we believe that eating was never intended to be a social event.

For the most part, the concept of eating to supply fuel and nutrients for the body seems to have gone by the wayside. How did this happen? One explanation is that over generations people gradually moved further away from eating foods in their original form and began eating more and more cooked, processed, and elaborately prepared foods. While cultural changes and modern methods of transportation led to the current trend of "eating on the run," science and technology responded with "convenience" foods and "fast" foods that are precooked, prepackaged, and treated with chemicals and preservatives. Now these foods are accepted as the norm, and this programming has become incorporated into our genes.

In many parts of the country if we tell someone we don't eat meat or we eat mostly fruits and vegetables, they frequently will respond with something like, "What are you, some kind of health nut?", as if it were strange. They seem to associate this approach to eating with certain cultural groups, rather than as a means for *anyone* to improve his or her health. How did we get so turned around in our thinking?

We've gotten so far away from eating foods in their original state that it's hard to find a restaurant that serves basic, unadulterated foods that aren't overcooked, masked by sauces, or made into concoctions. Some people actually find simple fruits and vegetables unappealing. This is only because their vehicles have become so accustomed to foods whose flavors have been buried by spices, sweeteners, seasonings, and sauces that their taste buds are dulled. How can we turn this around? The first step is to change the way we think!

We found that using different terminology was extremely helpful in changing the way we think about food. For example, using "fuel" instead of "food," and "consuming" instead of "eating" stimulated different responses from our vehicles.

"Consuming" and "fuel" aren't part of our old programming regarding eating; thus, they don't activate the same digestive and thinking processes. To illustrate this, all we have to do is think about "food" or that "it's time to eat," and the vehicle gets excited and says "Oh boy, food!" and the mouth starts to water. But this response doesn't happen when we use the words "consume" or "fuel" because they don't trigger the same programmed genetic impulses.

It always amazes us that the simplest techniques seem to yield the greatest results. For example, a very effective tool in changing our programming is to avoid ever saying "I'm hungry" or "I'm starved." First of all, the mind doesn't get hungry, so we know right off this is the vehicle talking (the voice of the genes). To say, "I'm really hungry," or "I'm starved," implies the need for large volumes of fuel, when in fact people say this out of habit, and it usually doesn't reflect a true need. So when the vehicle says, "I'm hungry," we (our minds) quickly step in and say, "Vehicle, you're *not* hungry. You're just a little low on energy and you could use some fuel." If the vehicle comes back with, "What do you mean? I'm starved!", we need to say more forcefully something like "Vehicle, you are *not* starved. I'm not going to listen to that. You simply need fuel."

In the beginning, the vehicle will probably continue to "argue back." For instance, after coming back from work, the vehicle might say, "Cookies! I need cookies!" And the mind says, "Now wait a second. You're going to have dinner in an hour. Cookies are full of sugar and they are harmful to your body. You don't need them." Then the vehicle comes back with "Just a couple can't hurt." But the mind rallies with "Don't give me that. I know if I let you eat one cookie, you'll eat a dozen." Then the genetic signals may try again to tempt you to give in, and without being conscious of it, your hand may be on the cookie jar. At this point the mind has to be strong and say, "Vehicle, stop! You don't need cookies. Everything is ok. Just relax. We're doing fine." This last example demonstrates how we sometimes also try to calm the vehicle, let it know we're on its side, and encourage it to cooperate with us. Each of us has to learn when a firm approach or a gentle approach yields the best results from our vehicle.

In a sense, when the "voice" of the old programming speaks up, it's like another person inside of us, or like a child, trying to convince us of something. But remember, no matter how loud the vehicle's voice gets, **the mind is stronger than the vehicle**. Every time we refuse to give in to what the vehicle wants to do, we build strength of mind. If we develop this strength, the next time the same habit response shows up, it is easier to control. The more we practice talking to the vehicle in this way, the stronger the stamp (programming) we make on the vehicle's genes. Our experience has shown that in time we can simply ignore the impulse from the vehicle and there's no need for dialog. In other words, as soon as the slightest hint of a desire for cookies enters the brain, the mind

can block it out without any argument from the vehicle. The only reason for any dialog is that we haven't yet learned how to keep the vehicle from getting its two cents in.

Checking Our Meter

We know the vehicle needs fuel. The question is, how much? How do we gauge how empty our "tank" is? Each of us has to become sensitive enough to develop our own meter--our own gauge for registering how full our tank is. It takes some trial and error to learn this. If we feel stuffed or sluggish after a meal, it means we allowed the vehicle to consume too much. Just like with a car, we don't want to fill our tank so full that there is no room for expansion.

As we first sit down to consume, it helps us to prepare the vehicle ahead of time by talking directly to it and saying (silently, of course), "Vehicle, I don't want you to consume any more fuel than you need." Then, periodically during the meal, we check our meters. In other words, we stop for a moment and ask, "Vehicle, have you had enough fuel?" If the response is an urge to consume more, then we need to examine if the vehicle really needs the fuel or if it just likes the taste. Going through this thought process is a way to help us (our minds) maintain our objectivity and consciously control how much we eat.

Likes and Dislikes

To be successful at reversing destructive eating habits, it is essential to gain some control over the vehicle's likes and dislikes. If a voice inside us says, "I hate vegetables," one way to respond is to say something like "That's not me, I refuse to accept that, I'm not going to listen to that anymore. That's the most ridiculous thing I've ever heard." By recognizing that it's our genes talking, it is easier to just laugh it off.

But merely blocking out the old programming isn't enough. It works best to replace it with new positive programming. In some cases, we found we had to con the vehicle in order to make it listen. For example, we might say, "Vehicle, vegetables are so good for you. I love vegetables. They're my favorite food." The funny thing is, this works. We've learned that if we say this with strength and believe it, in a short time the vehicle believes it as well. If the thought is programmed with enough repetition, eventually the voice of the genes' old programming starts to fade.

Automatic Pilot

The best way we know to break the vehicle's old habits regarding consuming is to *consciously* think and do everything in a different way. Until we put this principle into practice, we had no idea how much our vehicles functioned on "automatic pilot," that is, according to their old programming rather than being directed by the mind. Following are some examples demonstrating-how to do things differently from the way the vehicle would automatically do them.

If the vehicle is in the habit of sitting cross-legged, sit with your legs uncrossed. If you always hold the fork a certain way, hold it in your other hand or hold it a different way. If the vehicle always eats a handful of nuts at once, then eat just three or four nuts at a time. If it has to have something to eat shortly before going to bed, skip it once in a while. If it always saves the favorite food item for last, try eating it first next time. If the vehicle is in the habit of grabbing for the biggest piece of fruit, make a point to take the smallest one occasionally. If you make a lot of noise scraping your plate with a fork, try using restraint to prevent making so much noise.

We still have fun trying to zero in to the ways our vehicles do things, and consciously making them do as *we* (our minds) want them to. Turning this into a game seems to help us make bigger and faster strides in getting our minds more in control of our vehicles.

"Ultimate" Diets?

A major adjustment many of us had to make was relinquishing the idea of one particular diet being the only way to health. One person may be convinced that macrobiotics is the only way to health. Another person might believe the ultimate diet consists of fruit and nuts, whereas someone else might think a high protein diet with a lot of meat and dairy products is the healthiest way to eat.

Despite all the various opinions, we believe there is no "ultimate diet" for health that is appropriate for all humans, for all time. However, the Transfiguration Diet offers the finest formula we could arrive at for *these* vehicles in *this* environment, in *this* civilization, at *this* time.

As we evolve to a more refined condition and have greater control over our vehicles, and as we learn more about genetic reprogramming, doesn't it make sense that our diet would also need to evolve? For all we know, a single pill may be all that a more evolved human in some future generation might need to supply all its nutrition. We don't want to continue to be so primitive that we would be restricted or

limited by having cravings for a hamburger or a chocolate bar or a soda pop.

Extremes in Consuming

W ithin our own research team, we have witnessed significant and radical turn-arounds in individuals who had extreme consuming patterns. What do we mean by extreme? Anything that is done in excess in one direction or another is an extreme. Overconsuming, which leads to obesity; underconsuming, which can lead to anorexia nervosa; and bulimia are the most severe examples. But there are many less obvious consuming patterns that we also consider extremes. Some of these are: gorging for a few days followed by fasting, overeating at one meal and skipping another, eating three peanut butter sandwiches as a snack, eating half a box of chocolates, living almost exclusively on a few favorite foods, or stuffing ourselves at dinner until our stomachs are about to pop.

A ll of these are merely genetically triggered characteristics, whether they are inherited from our ancestors or programmed into our genes as a result of environmental influences. Remember, we are not responsible for the impulses we receive from the voice of our genes, but we are responsible for how we (our minds) respond to these influences and the degree of control we exert over them. It works best to simply look at the problem objectively, making no value judgment, and feeling no guilt or embarrassment. We all have our own package of genetically inherited weaknesses to deal with, and one person's is no better or worse than another's. Once we recognize that a problem exists (not wanting to eat, for example), and we understand the source, we must simply be determined to change and figure out a strategy that will work best to get control over the problem.

For example, let's say the vehicle doesn't want to eat because it is concerned with its figure. One way to reprogram the vehicle is to say, "Vehicle, you need more sustenance and weight on your bones. Don't worry, you're not going to get fat. You need to eat more if you are going to be well-nourished and healthy." If this approach doesn't work, then we just have to keep trying new approaches until we find one that does work. In this case, reprogramming that is directed more at the thinking behind the problem may be more effective. In other words, suppose the vehicle not only has deeply ingrained programming that "thin is beautiful," but it also is strongly influenced by environmental pressure that emphasizes the attractiveness of being "thin and trim." We might try saying, "Vehicle, you are so happy. You have no concern for your appearance. All you care about is what you are on the inside. Now stop worrying."

If the vehicle tries to come back with other negative programming such as, "I can't change," or "This is the way I am," or "It hasn't hurt me

yet," step in and say strongly, "There is NO truth to this, vehicle. You CAN change."

A very important point to keep in mind is that if we ever do permit the vehicle to get out of control and go on a binge of overconsuming or underconsuming, it's not the end of the world. It does no good to go on a downer, be discouraged, embarrassed, or feel any guilt. The only positive response is to **convert** the suffering we would have felt into **determination** to not let it happen again. We know from our own experiences that the vehicle's genetic impulses can be very strong at times. But we also know we (our minds) are stronger and we don't have to accept failure. Only through *practicing* the technique of genetic reprogramming can we build the strength of mind that makes each encounter with the vehicle's genetic impulses easier to handle.

A Two-Fold Approach

Interestingly, one of the advantages of the Transfiguration Diet is that as we became accustomed to the good taste of the healthful foods and the chemical balance they restored in our bodies, cravings for such things as sweets, meats, bread, coffee, and alcohol seemed to completely disappear. Even though many of us learned to successfully curb these cravings through the use of genetic reprogramming techniques, the impulses persisted in haunting us. We grew to know that some of the trouble we had with cravings was a result of chemical imbalances created by the poor quality foods we used to eat. After starting on this cleansing, healing diet, however, our tastes began to change. We required less and less food because we were receiving more nutrition from what we did eat, and as we eliminated more and more toxins from our bodies, the cravings for junk food disappeared. Now, it causes *no* reaction to walk past a bakery, or a hot dog stand, or an ice cream shop, except to say, "Yuk! I can't believe I used to eat that!"

The two-fold approach of combining genetic reprogramming with the Transfiguration Diet can put an end to the consuming roller coaster ride many of us have been on. Reprogramming our genes alone, or a healthy diet alone, may not be sufficient to totally free us from the vehicle's cravings. But we know the application of these two concepts together has *proven* to be remarkably successful.

three

"Yea" and "Nay" Foods

The "Nay's"--Foods to Avoid

Refined sugar, sugar products, artificial sweeteners
Dairy products: milk, butter, cheese, yogurt
Meat, fish
Eggs
Breads, flour products, commercial dry cereals
Processed foods, snack foods: chips, dips, soft drinks, frozen dinners, anything with added chemicals or food preservatives
Coffee, non-herbal teas
Fried foods
Excessive salt
Alcohol, tobacco

Sugar

Sugar and sugar products are frequently referred to as having "empty calories." There is no nutritive value contained in them; rather, they rob the vehicle of B-vitamins which are so important for the functioning of the nervous system. So many times we've observed individuals responding with tension, irritability, headaches, and nervousness immediately after consuming sugar. We hate to sound preachy, but sugar definitely is a "Nay" food that should be avoided. A little honey, sorghum or blackstrap molasses, or pure maple syrup can be used instead.

Mucus-Forming Foods

Dairy products, eggs, meat, flour products, and processed foods all have the effect of forming excessive mucus in the body. Instead of the thin, watery, healthy mucus that is normally present in the vehicle (body), lining the organs and tissues, consumption of these heavy mucus-forming foods makes it a thick, sticky substance that collects in the lymph system, blood vessels, sinuses, lungs, and all organs and tissues of the body. It causes congestion, stagnation, and a constipated condition throughout the entire organism.

The word "constipated" as used here does not apply only to the colon, but to the whole system when it is sluggish or clogged up. Our vehicles have the capacity to eliminate a certain amount of toxins and excessive mucus, but as individuals ingest more and more of the mucus-forming foods, the eliminative organs (skin, kidneys, lungs, colon) become overloaded. The body's natural response, in an effort to cleanse itself, is to periodically throw off the mucus in the form of colds, flu, and fever. Sometimes fever is the body's way of raising the temperature in order to liquefy the thick gluey mucus so it can be eliminated into the lymph and blood more easily.

Unfortunately, people often try to suppress these cold and flu symptoms, resulting in the waste material building up rather than being eliminated. If individuals continue to take in excessive food, chemicals, and other factors that serve no purpose in the body, the next step is for the body to accumulate and isolate the toxins and waste matter in the form of cysts, abscesses, skin disease, vaginal discharges, polyps, and tumors. It is called the process of "localization" and is part of the body's natural healing process to prevent premature breakdown of the whole vehicle (body).

We can't help but believe something is wrong when a doctor tells a woman, "Your mammogram (X-ray of the breasts) is normal," and in the next sentence says, "You have fibrocystic disease." What this means is that this disease (having multiple cysts in the breasts) is so *common* among women today that it is now being accepted as the *norm*. When the woman asks what she can do about it, the doctor may say that it helps to avoid caffeine and chocolate, but that's as far as many physicians are trained to go when it comes to nutrition counseling.

A couple of members of our Think Tank are nurses, one of whom works in the operating room. Her experiences helped open our eyes to other similar unhealthy conditions that are now being accepted as *normal*. For example, every day young children go to surgery to have "vent tubes" inserted into their eardrums to drain the pus and mucus that has collected in the middle ear. These children frequently also suffer with asthma, bronchitis, recurring colds or flu, tonsillitis, and throat infections. They are pitifully *congested*--which means their bodies are full of mucus and toxic poisons. One child was so clogged up that whenever he started to cry he would go into severe respiratory distress. He simply couldn't breathe. His mother apparently was afraid to let the child go and warned the nurse to be very careful if he started to cry. The nurse could hear the gurgling of the mucus in the throat and nose of the child, and yet the mother appeared to be totally unaware of what was causing the child's problem.

What's so unfortunate, is that because these symptoms are so prevalent, people come to accept them as normal. Parents call their children healthy when they are overweight, cranky, and have recurrent respiratory problems. But these are not normal, healthy conditions. Sweets, candy, soft drinks, processed foods of all kinds, meat, milk, and bread products are not foods for children. They need fruits, vegetables, nuts, seeds, fruit and vegetable juices, slow-

cooked whole grains--all the nutritious foods. This diet is not for adults only, but for our children as well. If we care for our children, why not give them foods that will let them grow up happy and healthy?

Toxic Colon

Mucus-forming substances adhere to the walls of the colon and over time form layer upon layer of dehydrated, compacted waste. Most people have literally pounds of fecal matter stored in their colon, toxifying their system and preventing nutrients from being assimilated through the colon wall. A combination of the gluey nature of the mucus and the narrowed diameter of the colon causes food to be slowed down in its passage through the colon. This results in more putrefaction (rotting) of the food. A good indication of putrefaction in the colon is bad breath and body or foot odor.

A doctor we know tells an enlightening story about body odor, from an experience he had while working 4 months in a Cambodian refugee camp. There was a severe water shortage--water had to be trucked in once a week. Since there was barely enough water to drink, the hygiene conditions were extremely primitive. Even though the people he treated rarely bathed, the doctor said he was amazed that no one had any body odor. In contrast, he felt the odor of the individuals he frequently encounters in American hospitals and emergency rooms is enough to knock him over. To us, this says a lot about the toxic condition that is created by a modern Western diet. The people in Cambodia, who had no access to refined and processed foods, and no opportunity to indulge in overconsuming, did not have the same toxic wastes and poisons stored in their bodies, and as a result, had none of the body odor that results from rotting waste.

It takes a long time to clean out a toxic colon and have it function as it should, even with a cleansing diet and herbs. We knew it would take a while after starting on the Transfiguration Diet before we would start assimilating all the nutrients from what we consume, so we do take vitamin and mineral supplements, as well as acidophilus, which restores the normal healthy bacteria to the colon.

Colonic irrigations have been helpful to some vehicles to accelerate the removal of mucus, parasites, and old fecal matter from the colon. There are a number of good books which explain colon health and colonic irrigations more thoroughly. If you are interested in having a colonic, check your yellow pages under "Colonic Irrigations" to find a clinic in your area.

The "Yea's"--Regenerative, Healthful Foods

Fruits and fruit juices
Vegetables and vegetable juices
Whole grains (low heated)
Raw nuts and seeds
Baked starchy vegetables (potatoes, sweet potatoes, winter squash)
Sprouts (alfalfa seeds, mung beans, wheat berries)
Natural sweeteners (honey, blackstrap molasses, pure maple syrup)
Unrefined, cold pressed oils (olive oil)

Live Grains

Whole grains such as wheat, barley, oats, and rye are very rich in protein, vitamins, minerals, and enzymes, but we only reap the benefit of these nutrients if we consume the grain in its whole live state. If the grain is pre-soaked 5 to 12 hours, then low heated in a food warmer-cooker (the type restaurants use) at a temperature of less than 130 degrees for 10 to 14 hours, the grain is soft, good tasting, and all the nutrients are in an organic state, which means they have *life* in them. One proof that the grains are still alive after slow cooking, is that they will grow if you plant them in the ground.

However, if the grain is ground to a fine powder, then heated to temperatures of up to 212 degrees or more, it becomes inorganic and there is no more life, or vitality, or healing qualities left in it. It is dead food, the enzymes being destroyed at temperatures above 130 degrees. After knowing this, it's hard to consider eating any form other than slow-cooked grains.

Preparing grains in this manner may sound like a lot of extra work at first, but it really isn't. Once we adjusted to a timing strategy that worked for us, it became a simple procedure that required very little effort. We found that we didn't need to pay any attention to the grain while it was cooking, and soon appreciated the fact that the little effort it does require is well worth it. More details on grain preparation and on how to use the food warmer-cooker are given in the *Recipes* section.

Mucusless Foods

Fruits, vegetables, fruit and vegetable juices, whole grains (low heated), nuts and seeds, sprouts, and unrefined, cold pressed oils make up what are called mucusless foods. Fruits, in particular, act as cleansers and work fast to break up mucus deposits. Vegetables are also cleansing, but to a lesser degree than fruit. They work well as an "intestinal broom" to sweep out the waste matter released into the colon. They

provide roughage, or fiber, and help rebuild the body. Grains, nuts, and seeds provide more protein, fat, and heat for the body. We use them more in colder weather or when doing strenuous physical exercise, since these are instances when our vehicles need more caloric energy than we'd get from just fruits and vegetables. Individuals who are trying to gain weight may also choose to consume more nuts and seeds.

If you are concerned about taste, we can honestly say we've never consumed such satisfying, good tasting food. We know that our tastes have changed considerably, and all the elaborate concoctions, sweets, and so-called "tasty" foods we used to eat no longer have any appeal to us.

Many combinations of salads can be made, although digestion is easier if the number of different vegetables used at one time is limited to four or five. Salad dressing made with olive oil, apple cider vinegar or lemon juice, garlic, and herbs is super tasting and very nutritious. We can be generous with the use of this salad dressing because of the quality of the ingredients it's made from. *Olive oil* is an excellent lubricant and specific cleanser for the liver and gall bladder. Apple cider vinegar (this is completely different from white distilled or wine vinegar which should not be used) contains malic acid, which aids in digestion. The *apple cider vinegar* supplies nutrients to strengthen the structure of arteries and veins, is high in potassium, has antiseptic qualities, breaks up mucus in the body, and much more. *Lemon juice* is a strong cleanser, a dissolver of mucus and toxins in the stomach and all parts of the body. It dissolves calcium deposits in the kidneys and joints and has been known to heal ulcers.

When cooking vegetables, the best method is to *steam them briefly*, adding herbs of your choice (for example, cloves, mustard, nutmeg, basil, thyme, savory, marjoram, cayenne, garlic, horseradish, curry, dill seed). Some of the mildly starchy vegetables like cauliflower and cabbage are actually easier to assimilate and have a sweet taste if they are steamed rather than raw. The true starchy vegetables, for example, potatoes and winter squash, shouldn't be eaten raw. The concentrated starch needs to be broken down in order for it to be digested properly. Potatoes and winter squash can be either steamed or baked, but we enjoy them best when they are baked. (Winter squash includes acorn squash, butternut squash, and pumpkin. Summer squash includes zucchini and yellow squash.)

Low-heated (slow-cooked) whole grains combined with vegetables and culinary herbs make a great casserole. The flavor can be varied by combining different vegetables with the grain and adding herbs (such as sweet basil, bay leaves, parsley, sage, thyme, savory, marjoram, cayenne, and garlic) and adding tamari, soy sauce, or Vege-Sal.

Raw vegetable juices are an excellent source of nutrition. They contain a concentrated amount of *live* vitamins, minerals, amino acids, enzymes, and salts the vehicle uses, and they are

digested and assimilated within 10 to 15 minutes after consuming them. Dr. N. W. Walker's book *Raw Vegetable Juices* goes into great detail on this subject.

The initial investment for buying a juicer may seem like a lot of money at first, but nothing can substitute for the healing quality of the live nutrients and "organic water" that you receive from fresh raw fruit and vegetable juices.

General Guidelines

Some basic healthy guidelines that we choose to follow in regard to consuming are:

1.   Chew food well, at least 20 times per bite. Some items, such as slow-cooked whole grains, require much more chewing.

2.   Be seated and relaxed when consuming, not in a hurry or walking around.

3.   Combine foods simply. Multiple food combinations are difficult if not impossible to digest. Fruits, for the most part, should be eaten alone, not at the same time you eat vegetables, protein, or starch. Wait at least 30 minutes after eating a fruit before eating other types of food.

4. Drink adequate water daily (distilled or spring water preferably). One to two quarts should be minimum for most people.

5. Avoid "washing down" what you consume with liquids. The liquid dilutes the digestive enzymes. It is best to wait at least 1 hour after consuming before drinking large quantities of liquids. It would be ok to have a small amount of water if taking something like vitamins.

6. Use sea salt or vegetable salt substitute instead of plain table salt. Be sure to keep salt consumption to a minimum.

7. Avoid extremes of temperatures. Steamed vegetables, baked potatoes, soup, and herbal teas should be served good and warm, but not so hot that they burn the roof of your mouth. It is also preferable to avoid drinking ice cold drinks.

8. Chew one type of food at a time during a meal; e.g., chew a bite of potato separately from a bite of steamed vegetable or salad.

9. Taste your food first before automatically adding seasonings to it. You especially want to avoid adding soy sauce or Vege-Sal out of habit, since you are trying to limit your salt intake.

Making the Transition

We cannot stress enough that it can be dangerous to immediately change from a standard meat, milk, and bread diet to a cleansing, mucusless diet without going through a period of transition. As soon as you stop adding mucus-forming foods, chemicals, and other toxins into your vehicle and replace them with cleansing foods, the vehicle will begin to eliminate the old accumulated waste at an accelerated rate. If this dumping of toxins from all the body tissues into the blood happens too rapidly, it can poison the system and make you feel quite ill.

We want to be sure you understand that this diet *will* bring toxins to the surface, whether it is in the form of colds and flu, skin rashes or pimples, unusual discharges, aches and pains, or just having some days when you feel low on energy. This is how the cleansing process works. It is *supposed* to happen. Don't be alarmed and don't give up. These symptoms only prove that your body has some house cleaning to do. By eliminating all the "Nay" Foods, your body will be able to begin healing itself. It may help you to remain encouraged and have a positive attitude if you read some other books that discuss the "cleansing crisis" in more detail. Two books we recommend are *Mucusless-Diet Healing System* by Prof. Arnold Ehret, and *Dr. Christopher's Three-Day Cleansing Program, Mucusless Diet, and Herbal Combinations* by Dr. John R. Christopher. It really does give added support to understand the principles involved in the cleansing process.

J ust don't be surprised if you do have some rough days. The good days *will* come soon, and they will be better than any good days you knew previously.

I t is best to make the transition gradually over a few days to a couple of weeks. This transition will be different for every individual depending on the vehicle's constitution and what it has been previously consuming. It would be safe for anyone to cut back or even eliminate sugar, processed foods, dairy products, and red meat, as a start. Then gradually increase your consumption of whole foods like fruits and steamed or raw vegetables, while you slowly eliminate the other mucus-forming and processed foods. However, if this is drawn out too much, the danger or temptation of not completing the transition can become a problem.

I f you are not familiar with the cleansing process, we suggest you check with a physician or someone who is familiar with purification and detoxification procedures. Thank goodness, the AMA and some doctors are finally beginning to realize the value of nutrition and are incorporating it into their practice. More and more doctors are joining hands with nutritionists in order to provide their patients with a broader program for improved health. If you happen to live in an area where you find no nutritional guidance

from a physician, try to seek out other health care professionals who have knowledge in wholistic medicine. Sometimes you can use health food stores, clinics, herb shops, wholistic health centers, and even the yellow pages as a resource for finding someone knowledgeable in the area of nutrition.

Changing the type of foods we eat has a definite effect on our digestive processes. One of the most frequent comments we hear is that when eating more raw foods, some individuals experience gas and bloating. This temporary condition only happens because the raw foods stir up old accumulated wastes in the colon, and this creates gas. Remember how we referred to vegetables previously as an "intestinal broom?" Actually, the gas then serves a purpose in moving the contents of the colon along. We know this can be very uncomfortable at times--but just know that this phase will pass. If you are one who gets frequent gas pains, it can be a sign you may be making your transition too fast. You may need to consume more steamed or baked vegetables and cooked grains, and less raw fruits and vegetables.

One remedy for gas pains is to drink some catnip and fennel seed tea or take some drops of catnip fennel tincture. If you have some fennel seed capsules available, take them; or for even faster re-lief, empty the contents of 2 to 4 capsules into some hot water and drink it. We wish we would have known these tricks when we first started on the diet instead of learning the hard way. We hope these little hints will help you.

It might also help to know that while your body is repairing itself, it uses up more energy. This accounts for some of the weakness, or lack of energy, you may feel at first. We found it took approximately 8 weeks before most of us felt our energy level had stabilized. During this period it may be helpful to get a little extra rest if you need it.

A Total Lifestyle Change

We want to emphasize that what we are really talking about is a new way of life. This isn't simply a temporary reducing diet, or a diet you plan to follow for a couple of months and then return to your old eating habits. The cleansing, healing process cannot work if you repeatedly go back and forth between the Transfiguration Diet and your previous pattern of consuming. It doesn't work to say, "Well, I'll just have this one small pizza. I haven't had one in two months, it can't hurt me."

We have learned from experience that the best results come from sticking to the new diet 100% and making it a part of our lifestyle. Luckily, as a result of our practice in applying the technique of reprogramming our genes, we were able to make this change without much difficulty. We hope that by sharing these tools with you, you can do the same.

Transition Diet

To give you an example of how to make the transition, the first step our research group took was to eliminate all sugar products, dairy products, bread, red meat, and processed foods from our diet. In the morning, we consumed lightly salted oatmeal with a teaspoon of honey and a teaspoon of raisins (no milk or butter). Old-fashioned 100% rolled oats is probably the closest to a whole grain cereal of all the cereal products available on the market today. If you prepare oatmeal, cook it on a low-heat setting and do not overcook it. As soon as you have the needed equipment, you can replace the oatmeal with slow-cooked whole grains.

For the noon meal, we prepared a raw vegetable salad and steamed new potatoes. We experimented with a variety of vegetables (lettuce, spinach, green peppers, cucumbers, scallions, cauliflower, broccoli, carrots, peas, summer squash, green beans) and added alfalfa seed sprouts or mung bean sprouts (homegrown or purchased from a store) and sunflower seeds. Cauliflower was the only vegetable that was generally agreed to be less tolerable raw. We also tried lentil and azuki bean sprouts, but they seemed to be too gas forming in the colon. Alfalfa sprouts seemed to be the most compatible and digestible with the salad. We soon learned that the *simpler* the food combinations, the more easily digestible they are. By limiting our salad to four or five different vegetables, it was easier for our systems to digest.

It is true that different altitudes and environments will also have an effect on the way our vehicles (bodies) respond to certain foods. Some individuals discovered when traveling, for example, that azuki and mung bean sprouts did not have the same gas-producing effect when consumed in different parts of the country. So, we believe our locale may play a role in determining which foods are more compatible with our vehicles.

The new potatoes were excellent during this transition, because so many individuals found that they craved starch and something heftier than just salad. Then, as the vehicles began to adjust to the diet, the craving for starch and the desire for bulk gradually subsided.

For the evening meal, the transition period was a good opportunity to prepare some of the leftover items in our refrigerator or pantry. Turkey, chicken, pinto beans, and rice are possible transitional consuming items. As an example, we tried preparing two steamed vegetables along with one of the other items (white meat, rice, or beans).

We chose to have the heavier meal in the evening, but you can have it at noon if that works better with your schedule. However, it is best to have the heavier meal at the same time every day, to keep your vehicle from having to make constant adjustments.

Within a few days to a week, we began to prepare evening meals that consisted of one baked starchy vegetable (Irish potato, sweet potato, acorn squash, butternut squash, pumpkin), along with two steamed vegetables (one green and one yellow or non-green), and a vegetable salad made primarily of lettuce and spinach. We don't know what you might like, but of the starchy vegetables, the baked potato has always been the most satisfying to us.

A baked potato is very good with some added garlic oil, fresh chopped parsley or lightly steamed chopped green pepper, cayenne or fresh ground black pepper, and some soy sauce or Vege-Sal on it. You can add any one or combination of these seasonings that you would enjoy. Eventually, you may find, as we did, that you enjoy the potato taste better if you just add a generous amount of garlic oil and some soy sauce. Note that much of the nutrient content of the potato is within the 1/4 inch closest to the skin. If you scrub the potatoes well before baking, and check for bad spots as you consume them, then you can eat all or part of the skin along with the potato.

We initially steamed our vegetables until they were quite tender. After a few months, we reduced the cooking time so they had some crispness left in them at serving time. Less cooking preserves more of the nutrients, and we actually enjoy the flavor more when they are less cooked. When steamed to the right tenderness, still having some crispness left in them, the vegetables should be a brilliant color. If you steam them any longer, you will see the color begin to fade (which means the nutrients are being destroyed as well).

four

Three-Day Juice "Squeeze"

After a few days to a week on the transitional diet, we began our Transfiguration Diet with a three-day juice cleanse. The purpose of the juice cleanse is to detoxify or purify the body by accelerating the loosening up or dissolving of mucus buildup, and replacing the toxins and acid materials that are eliminated with the alkaline fruit juice. In a sense you can think of this process as "squeezing" out the toxic poisons. An important concept to understand is that when you choose to undergo this new way of consuming, your primary purpose is not to obtain the maximum nutritive value from foods. This will be amply provided anyway. The primary purpose is to restore tissues to a healthy condition and improve the body's assimilation of what you consume through the *cleansing*, *healing*, and *rebuilding* qualities of the food.

This is why so many individuals on this diet gradually require less and less food; they are able to assimilate a greater percentage of the nutrients. Many individuals on a heavy starch and meat diet can consume such large quantities and still be hungry, because they aren't able to absorb the nutrients they take in. So when counting up the amount of protein, minerals, vitamins, and amino acids you consume, remember that it depends largely on *how clean your colon is* as to how many of these nutrients you are absorbing.

One three-day cleanse will in no way clean out all the mucus in the body. A continual program of periodic cleansing, mucusless foods, fasting, and herbs will do so, but it may take a few years. You will, however, feel a measurable difference immediately after the first juice cleanse, and a steady improvement from that time on.

As we mentioned earlier, be prepared for some difficult days when your body goes through what is called a "cleansing crisis," when it is trying to push out a lot of mucus at once. It can be in the form of mucus drainage from your head or chest, constipation, or aches and pains in areas which have given you trouble in the past. It is temporary, so there's nothing to fear. It is really something to be happy about because it's a good sign that you are in the healing process.

One thing we learned was to avoid contact with others who have colds, flu, or other symptoms, until we were far enough into the transition for our immune systems to make adjustments to this diet. Some individuals seemed to have less resistance and defenses to protect them until their immune systems were built up. However, we also discovered that once we'd been on the diet just a short while, the severity of any symptoms were much less.

Again, you can expect your initial adjustment to the diet to take about eight weeks before you feel your energy level to be most consistent, and your weight to be stabilized. *You will lose weight* during the three-day cleanse and probably during the first few weeks of the Transfiguration Diet as well. Those of you who are more overweight will probably continue to lose gradually until you arrive at the correct weight for your vehicle, even while you consume as much as you want of the right foods. Those who are thin and don't really want to lose more weight can maintain their weight by consuming more baked potatoes, more grains, more oils, and more nuts and seeds.

Directions and Guidelines

1. Upon arising, **drink 16 ounces of prune juice**. The purpose of the prune juice is to draw waste matter from all parts of the body into the colon, as well as to empty the colon.

2. **Follow this 30 minutes later with 8 ounces of apple juice. Then take another 8 ounces of apple juice every 30 minutes.** Periodically, you can substitute distilled water in place of the juice, a few sips or up to 8 ounces. The **goal is to drink approximately 1 gallon of the apple juice during the day.** This is in addition to the 16 ounces of prune juice and any water you drink. The 1 gallon is an approximation. A general rule is to **drink no more than 1 ounce of apple juice per pound of body weight**. Someone weighing 95 pounds would not drink more than 95 ounces of juice. Someone weighing 180 pounds may drink more than 1 gallon if he tolerates it well (1 gallon equals 128 ounces). Allow 30 minutes between each dose of apple juice or water. It helps to keep a written record of the amount of juice you drink.

3. **Use the same type juice for the entire 3 days**. Grape juice, carrot juice, or citrus juice (if you are in a citrus growing region) can be used in place of apple juice, depending on what is more compatible with your vehicle. If you begin by

using apple juice and after a day or two find it incompatible, then you may still switch to another type of juice. If you use grape juice, dilute it half and half with distilled water. **Use fresh juice you prepare yourself or 100% natural bottled juice that has no additives or preservatives in it.** Do not use frozen juice concentrates, or bottled juice that has water or sugar added.

4. **"Chew" your juice** well by swishing it thoroughly around in your mouth. You will get much more nutritional and cleansing value from it if it mixes well with the saliva.

5. Don't attempt to force more juice down if your stomach can't handle it. Skip a drink now and then and **try pushing up against your diaphragm (in the center of your chest) to push air bubbles out of the stomach.** You can determine your own schedule of how often to take juice or water depending on the total amount you have to consume each day.

6. **Avoid drinking juice later than 1-1/2 hours before you go to bed** to prevent juice from remaining in your stomach and possibly causing nausea.

7. **Take some olive oil** to lubricate the liver and bile ducts. Older or larger vehicles can take 1-1/2 to 2 tablespoons 3 times a day. Younger or smaller

vehicles can take 1 to 1-1/2 tablespoons 3 times a day.

8.   The breaking up of mucus that will empty into the colon generally results in constipation during the cleanse, if no action is taken to prevent it. It is very important to **keep the colon eliminating properly**. Once in the morning is not enough. You should empty the colon at least 2 or 3 times a day. An herbal formula prepared by Dr. Christopher called Naturalax II can assist in keeping the colon functioning. It worked for us to start out with 2 capsules 3 times a day, then we increased or decreased the dosage according to our body's needs. Naturalax II is mild and takes several hours to take effect. It is food for the colon and is not something you will become dependent on. Naturalax can be taken with one of your 8-ounce glasses of water or juice. You may also **take more prune juice if constipated**. If you have had no colon elimination by 1 pm the first day, drink 16 ounces more prune juice. Some individuals will expel a lot of liquid from the colon along with the waste. Do not be alarmed. That is normal during the cleanse.

9.   **We didn't take any drugs** such as aspirin, acetaminophen, buffered aspirin, or antacids after starting the three-day cleanse. There are herbal formulas for headaches or intestinal gas that can give relief without adding unwanted chemicals to the body. An interesting question I once read

regarding this was, "Why would you take aspirin for a headache? Is it because your body is deficient in aspirin?" Well, of course it is not. The point is that the cleansing diet and herbs will treat the cause and not just the symptoms of disease the way many drugs do. However, we are not saying that there are no circumstances when these drugs might be needed. If you are having severe pain, whether it be from an injury, having dental work done, or a headache, for example, we recommend you follow the advice of a physician or other qualified health care professional.

First Day Off the Fast

1. Upon arising, drink 16 ounces of prune juice.

2. At least 30 minutes later, or anytime in the morning, consume 1/2 apple with a carrot and raisins, or 1 or 2 of the same kind of fruit.

3. At noon, have a combination raw vegetable salad (no sunflower seeds, nuts, potatoes, or grain).

4. For the evening meal, consume a raw vegetable salad, a couple of steamed vegetables, and a small baked potato.

5.   During the day, you can consume fruit or vegetable juices, fresh or dried fruits, carrot and celery sticks. Avoid concentrated foods like nuts and seeds.

6.   ** HOLD VOLUME DOWN. ** Avoid over-consuming.

7.   ** KEEP YOUR COLON WORKING. ** If you have not eliminated anything from your colon by early afternoon, drink more prune juice. Take an enema if you have had no results by late afternoon. Keep your Naturalax II intake up. The mucus and wastes that have been loosened during the fast collect in the colon and much of it won't be shed until **after** the fast when you start to consume fruits and vegetables. As was mentioned previously, the vegetables in particular serve as an intestinal broom to sweep the area clean.

8.   Proceed with the Starter Diet on the second day.

five

Our Starter Diet

Morning

Fresh Fruit or Low-Heated Whole Grains

Either fruit or grain is perfectly acceptable for the morning meal. There may be days when your body seems to require something more substantial, and the grain will sustain you better and be more satisfying than just fruit. However, you may also find, as we have, that on some days fruit alone will be all you want and will make an adequate and satisfying meal.

Fruits are *best* when they are in season and locally grown, but this is not always possible. We have found a variety of fruits to be acceptable in the temperate climate we are in: apples, pears, bananas, cherries, grapes, peaches, pineapple, nectarines, plums, melons, fresh or frozen berries (strawberries, blueberries, blackberries, raspberries, boysenberries). Frozen berries are fine as long as no sugar syrups have been added.

We know most people don't have easy access to organic fruits, but there is some concern for the pesticides, chemicals, and wax that may be on the skins. One way to eliminate the problem is to peel the fruit if you choose.

Although we will occasionally consume citrus fruits (oranges, grapefruit, tangerines, lemons, limes) they are actually best if you are in a warm or tropical climate. Even if you are in a warm climate, but move from air-conditioned house to air-conditioned car to air-conditioned work place, you are in an artificial environment that doesn't match a citrus-fruit climate.

For cereal grains, we enjoy whole oats and wheat berries the best. The slow-cooked whole grains can be eaten as is, or, since they require a lot of chewing, you may enjoy them more after blending them briefly in a blender or food processor until they are about the consistency of oatmeal. They are much easier to digest this way and there seems to be more flavor. The blended wheat has a rich wheat germ taste.

The grains can be sweetened with 1 tsp. of honey or 1 to 2 tsp. of pure maple syrup per bowl. Pure maple syrup is available in grades A through C. Grade C is the least refined and therefore has more nutritive value. If you can't find the graded types, any pure maple syrup will be fine. You can also add 1 to 2 tsp. of raisins or some diced apple to the cereal grain. Or, you might try sprinkling cinnamon on the grain, either alone with the honey, or together with the raisins or diced apple. More information on grain preparation is given in the *Recipes* section.

You should know that the end product of cooking the grains can be somewhat unpredictable when you first start preparing them. If they are not soaked at cool temperatures (in the refrigerator is best), or if the cooking temperature drops too low or gets too high, it is possible for the grains to ferment slightly. Don't worry! This is normal. You will quickly become familiar with your equipment and the temperature controls and will learn what adjustments to make to prevent this from happening. If the cereal grain does ferment, then this would be a good day to have fruit for your first meal. Note that we would not recommend that you eat the grain if it is fermented.

Noon

Green Salad with Live Grain Casserole

For our noon vegetable salad, the combination we chose includes lettuce, spinach, cucumber, and broccoli, with optional grated carrots (enough to add color), alfalfa sprouts, and green peas. We add green peas if we're not consuming peas in the grain casserole or at the evening meal that day.

Variations of the grain casserole (low-heated grains combined with vegetables and seasonings) can be found in the *Recipes* section. Once you have your timing strategy worked out, you will find these casseroles easy to prepare and convenient to have available, whether you eat your noon meal at home or take a lunch with you to work or school.

Another option that is very satisfying at the noon meal, especially if you are short on time for preparing grain casserole, is to have some Littlegreen Potato Soup. We think this is the best soup we ever had. It is made using distilled water, vegetable broth powder, potatoes, vegetables, herbs, and seasonings. Some brands of vegetable broth powder are called "potassium broth" because of the high quantity of potassium in the dehydrated vegetables. "Bernard Jensen's Broth or Seasoning" is the brand we primarily use, and

you can get it at your health food store. We also prepare this soup any time someone needs soft or liquid food, such as after going to the dentist or when having a fever or flu symptoms. It contains lots of garlic, which is a natural antibiotic, and the soup is very nutritious as well as satisfying. Refer to the *Recipes* section for details on how to prepare it.

Evening

Salad, Steamed Vegetables, Baked Potato

In the raw vegetable salad we prepare for the evening meal, we use only lettuce and spinach in order to provide more green leafy vegetables while keeping our total food combinations to a minimum.

We also prepare one green and one yellow or non-green steamed vegetable. The green vegetables that we think are good when steamed are broccoli, cabbage, green peas, green beans, baby limas, zucchini squash, asparagus, and artichokes. The yellow or non-green vegetables we use are yellow squash, corn on the cob, carrots (with celery and/or mung bean sprouts), cauliflower and beets. We experimented with other vegetables not mentioned in these lists. Some of these vegetables, like steamed okra or eggplant, are fine if you don't find them objectionable. If fresh vegetables are not available, some frozen vegetables are acceptable (for example, peas, corn, or baby limas). The *Recipes* section describes how to prepare each of these steamed vegetables and presents some ideas for seasoning.

We didn't mention the leafy green vegetables such as spinach and watercress in our steamed vegetable list because we only consume them raw. The dark leafy green vegetables are rich in oxalic acid, which is very beneficial to the body in its natural live state. However, if they are cooked, the oxalic acid becomes inorganic and combines with other elements to form oxalic acid crystals that can be deposited in the kidneys. We like spinach raw in salads and vegetable juice, so see no reason to ever cook it.

We really enjoy a baked potato at the evening meal. To season it, try adding a generous amount of garlic oil (as much as you want) and some tamari or soy sauce. For variety, you can add fresh chopped parsley or steamed chopped green pepper, cayenne or fresh ground black pepper, or Vege-Sal. We recommend not using Vege-Sal and tamari or soy sauce at the same time because of the high salt content in each. It also doesn't make much sense to us to use cayenne and black pepper at the same time since they are so similar.

Sweet basil, thyme, caraway seed, and celery seed are some examples of the season-

ing herbs that act as carminatives (relieve flatulency or gas in the stomach and intestines). We frequently add one of these herbs to our raw vegetable salads, and use them as seasoning in the steamed vegetables. Cloves are also carminative and are tasty in steamed carrots.

Snacks

Vegetable juices

Fruit juices: primarily apple, grape, or prune juice (these are bottled juices that are 100% pure and natural without added water or sugar)

Fresh fruits: as listed in the MORNING section

Dried fruits (unsulphured): apricots, currants, prunes, and raisins

Carrot and celery sticks

Raw nuts and seeds (not salted or roasted): almonds, cashews, walnuts, pecans, and sunflower seeds

Supplements

Cayenne

Start by taking 1/4 teaspoon of this herb 3 times a day. Gradually work up to 1 teaspoon 3 times a day. Dissolve the cayenne in 4 to 6 ounces of distilled water. Drink this, then chase it with more distilled water. Cayenne is a pure stimulant, increasing the functional activity and energy in the body. It is a specific food for the heart and blood vessels and helps them regain their elasticity. It equalizes the blood circulation throughout the whole body, thus is valuable for any hemorrhage (whether internal or external), and for restoring normal blood pressure. Cayenne heals stomach and intestinal ulcers, stimulates the peristaltic motion of the intestines, has antiseptic qualities, and much more. Cayenne is the strongest of the three categories of Capsicum (paprika, red pepper, and cayenne). Any Capsicum that has over 25 BTU's (British thermal units) is classified as cayenne. At times you can purchase cayenne with as much as 10,000 BTU's, so decrease your dosage if it is too strong (too hot) for your particular vehicle. To assure that you get good quality cayenne, we recommend that you buy it at a health food store.

Apple Cider Vinegar

 T ake 1 tablespoon 3 times a day. It can be taken immediately after the cayenne. Take it straight, or add a little water if you find it necessary to dilute it. Some individuals can tolerate it better when they first start using it if it is mixed with a little honey. Use only apple cider vinegar, which contains malic acid, as opposed to white distilled or white wine vinegar, which contains harmful acetic acid. Heinz is one good brand of pure apple cider vinegar that you can buy at most supermarkets. Be sure not to get "cider-flavored" vinegar. Apple cider vinegar dissolves mucus, has anti-septic qualities, aids in proper coagulation of blood, builds healthy blood vessels, and aids in digestion.

Kelp Tablets

 T ake 2 tablets daily. Individuals with a malfunctioning thyroid gland could use more. It replaces salt, is rich in iodine and other minerals, and helps rebuild the thyroid gland. You can find kelp tablets in any health food store and in some supermarkets.

Blackstrap Molasses or Sorghum

 T ake 1 tablespoon 3 times a day. It provides an abundant and easily assimilated form of calcium, potassium, and iron. We have found Plantation brand to be a good quality blackstrap molasses, and it can be purchased in health food stores. Be sure to get *unsulphured* molasses.

Wheat Germ Oil

Take 1 tablespoon 3 times a day. This is a rich source of fatty acids, vitamin E, and octacosanol. Vitamin E is believed to play a role in stimulating the immune system, preventing formation of abnormal blood clots, and it is an anti-oxidant; it prevents oils from becoming rancid. Octacosanol is believed to be the agent in wheat germ oil that provides the energy-giving effects (improving endurance and vitality, and speeding reaction time). Wheat germ oil can be found in most health food stores.

Some individuals' schedules may require that they take 1-1/2 tablespoons of molasses and wheat germ oil 2 times a day instead of 1 tablespoon 3 times a day.

"Goodies"

On holidays or special occasions, we like to prepare some special treats that are fun and tasty while still being healthy and nutritious.

If you substitute fresh or unsweetened frozen blackberries, blueberries, boysenberries, strawberries, or raspberries on your cereal grains, you have a delightful meal. Or, dried currants can make a good tasting substitute for raisins.

We prepare our own almond butter in a Champion juicer. You can also make your own cashew and other nut butters or buy them in a health food store. The almonds are not as oily as some other nuts, so you have to add olive oil when putting them through the juicer. (Refer to your juicer manual before attempting to make the nut butters.) You may also want to add a little sea salt to bring out the flavor. Besides being fun to make, these nut butters make super tasting spreads on carrot and celery sticks and sliced apple.

If you want to make something that looks and tastes more like candy, try preparing some raisin-nut balls. In a blender, chop up a mixture of raisins or currants with almonds, cashews, pecans, and walnuts. If the proportion of raisins to nuts is about 50/50, you can easily roll the chopped mixture into balls and they will hold together well. You can add other items for flavoring, such as vanilla or almond extract, cinnamon, allspice, and honey. Place the raisin-nut balls in the freezer to chill before serving.

Baked apples are good when you'd like something sweet and warm. Our favorite method of preparing baked apples is to add cinnamon, whole cloves, allspice, honey, and currants. First core the apple, but not all the way through. You want to leave one end closed so the honey and raisins won't pour out the bottom during baking. Peel the top third of the apple. Insert cloves into the peeled section. Sprinkle with cinnamon and allspice. Put 2 teaspoons currants into the hole and pour 2 teaspoons honey over the currants and around the top of the apple. Bake at 350 degrees for 1 hour.

For a specialty beverage, you can serve Welch's nonalcoholic Sparkling Grape Juice that comes in bottles resembling wine or champagne, or prepare some hot apple juice (2/3 apple juice to 1/3 distilled water) and serve it with cinnamon sticks or sprinkle ground cinnamon on it.

Tips for Travelers

You can easily adhere to this diet, and even maintain all your supplements, while traveling. Surprisingly, the only difficulty is taking down the names and addresses of all the people you encounter who are so fascinated by what you are consuming, that they want to learn about it and start on the diet themselves.

Simply take along containers with your supplements, salad dressing, garlic oil, and tamari or soy sauce wherever you go. A small travel bag with a shoulder strap allows you to carry these items easily whether you are traveling in a car, on a plane, or walking into a restaurant. There are several food establishments that have salads, or a salad bar, and serve baked potatoes. (Cafeterias, Wendy's, Western Sizzlin' Steak House, and the Sizzler Steak House are some examples.) When traveling by plane, remember to order a *pure* vegetarian plate at the time you make your reservation. If you don't specify "pure", you may be served eggs, cheese, milk, or breads.

As you are seated in a restaurant or on a plane, have no hesitation to take out your cayenne, apple cider vinegar, molasses, wheat germ oil, and take your supplements before consuming. If you don't have enough time to allow some spacing between your supplements (to allow for proper food combining), just go ahead and take them one after the other. When selecting foods at a cafeteria or salad bar, keep in mind to limit the varieties of foods. Avoid concoctions made with mayonnaise, cheese sauces, other types of vinegar, salted nuts and seeds, and avoid the commercial salad dressings.

Littlegreen Restaurants/Cafeterias

Some of us who worked on writing this book started out on this diet by going to each other's houses and taking turns preparing meals. It provided an opportunity for us to learn new ideas and experiment with various ways to prepare the food, while being in a supportive environment. Even though this was helpful to us, it was also awkward at times, and it is not a method that could work practically or satisfactorily for everyone.

We know it can be extremely difficult to change your eating habits without the support of others in your household or at your work place. It can create a very stressful situation at times. For those who start out on this new diet, it would be ideal if you had a place to go where you could get three meals a day if you chose, or go for a lunch break from work. It would be ideal if you had a place to go when traveling away from home. But in most cities in this country, there is not one public place you can go to that provides this type of food

(low-heated whole grains, briefly steamed vegetables, pure salad dressings, and so forth).

We feel that what is desperately needed is to open up Littlegreen Restaurants or Cafeterias. We would love to see at least one in every major city. We hope to eventually be a part of such a venture, although it has not yet been financially feasible for us. If we find that it's truly wanted, it might happen sooner than we think. Since this diet is such a radical approach to consuming, compared to the typical American diet, such a restaurant may not be a money-making venture. However, even if it just supported itself, it would be worth the effort, for it would provide a tremendous service.

Menus/Sample Consuming Schedules

The following menus and sample consuming schedules are guides to assist you in getting started on the Transfiguration Diet. The menus present some ideas as to which foods can be combined to make meals, and demonstrates ways of rotating different foods.

At the morning meal, for example, you could consume just fruit, or you could have wheat or oats with one of a selection of fruits and a natural sweetener. The noon meal generally consists of a raw vegetable salad, with the addition of either a grain casserole or Littlegreen Potato Soup. For the evening meal, the menu gives some suggested combinations of green and yellow or non-green vegetables. If you wonder why we don't include all the possible vegetables that would be acceptable, we wanted to give you a more accurate representation of the choices we found to be the best tasting and most satisfying during the early phases of this diet. If you like steamed okra or eggplant, for example, then by all means, feel free to consume them.

Likewise, we only list Irish potatoes for the baked starchy vegetable at the evening meal. Although we alternated with winter squash (acorn squash, butternut squash, pumpkin) for a time, we consistently found that the Irish potato seemed to supply what our vehicles needed and wanted.

We want to emphasize that all the items and the ways they are listed will not necessarily be maintained on a permanent basis. After a period of time on the diet, you will naturally advance to consuming less cooked food. This should occur gradually, however. There's no need to rush it. If you're like us, your body will automatically want less and less morning grain or need it less often, and be satisfied with just fruit. Or, you will automatically start wanting more raw vegetable salad and less grain casserole or steamed vegetables. Instead of craving two potatoes, you'll probably reach a point of needing only one or just half a potato. So don't be surprised to see this change happen. Even as we write this book, changes in our diet are advancing so quickly

that we expect there will be a phase II of the Transfiguration Diet.

The sample consuming schedules give actual daily accounts of what two individuals on the Transfiguration Diet consumed. You'll notice Schedule A reflects an amount that might be consumed by someone with a regular appetite who is at an acceptable weight for his vehicle's size. Schedule B demonstrates what a thin person who is trying to gain weight might consume. From this chart, you can also see examples of the time spacing that is allowed between consuming different foods, such as the 10 to 15 minute gap between supplements, or the minimum 1-1/2 to 2 hour gap after consuming the morning grains.

You may later reach a stage, as we did, when you'll want to do a one-day fast each week. We recommend that you begin any fasting only *after* you've solidly adjusted to the Transfiguration Diet. It may be as soon as 8 weeks (not sooner), or you may not feel ready for fasting until you've been on the diet for 5 to 6 months. Fasting does accelerate the cleansing, healing process and also gives your digestive system a rest. You can choose to fast on distilled water alone, or have fruit juice diluted half and half with distilled water, or drink herb teas. To avoid constipation from developing as a result of dissolved toxic wastes and mucus being dumped into the colon, either drink some prune juice or take Naturalax II--the herbal lower bowel tonic.

MENU CYCLE ONE

	SUN	MON	TUE	WED	THU	FRI	SAT
	Wheat Berries *Honey & Raisins or Apple (opt) or Fruit	Wheat Berries *Honey & Raisins or Apple (opt) or Fruit	Oats *Honey & Raisins or Apple (opt) or Fruit	Wheat Berries *Honey & Raisins or Apple (opt) or Fruit	Wheat Berries *Honey & Raisins or Apple (opt) or Fruit	Oats *Honey & Raisins or Apple (opt) or Fruit	Wheat Berries *Honey & Raisins or Apple (opt) or Fruit
	Lettuce, Spinach, Cucumber & Broccoli Salad Sprouts, Carrots, Peas (opt) Potato Soup	Lettuce, Spinach, Cucumber & Broccoli Salad Sprouts, Carrots (opt) Rye Casserole	Lettuce, Spinach, Cucumber & Broccoli Salad Sprouts, Carrots (opt) Barley Casserole	Lettuce, Spinach, Cucumber & Broccoli Salad Sprouts, Carrots (opt) Barley Casserole	Lettuce, Spinach, Cucumber & Broccoli Salad Sprouts, Carrots (opt) Barley Casserole	Lettuce, Spinach, Cucumber & Broccoli Salad Sprouts, Carrots (opt) Rye Casserole	Lettuce, Spinach, Cucumber & Broccoli Salad Sprouts, Carrots, Peas (opt) Barley Casserole
	Lettuce/Spinach Salad Irish Potato Beets Green Beans	Lettuce/Spinach Salad Irish Potato Carrots/Celery Broccoli	Lettuce/Spinach Salad Irish Potato Corn Green Peas	Lettuce/Spinach Salad Irish Potato Yellow Squash Cabbage	Lettuce/Spinach Salad Irish Potato Cauliflower Zucchini Squash	Lettuce/Spinach Salad Irish Potato Corn Broccoli	Lettuce/Spinach Salad Irish Potato Carrots/Celery Cabbage

*See enlarged options under "Goodies" section

MENU CYCLE TWO

	SUN	MON	TUE	WED	THU	FRI	SAT
Breakfast	Wheat Berries *Honey & Raisins or Apple (opt) or Fruit	Wheat Berries *Honey & Raisins or Apple (opt) or Fruit	Oats *Honey & Raisins or Apple (opt) or Fruit	Wheat Berries *Honey & Raisins or Apple (opt) or Fruit	Wheat Berries *Honey & Raisins or Apple (opt) or Fruit	Oats *Honey & Raisins or Apple (opt) or Fruit	Wheat Berries *Honey & Raisins or Apple (opt) or Fruit
Lunch	Lettuce, Spinach, Cucumber & Broccoli Salad *Sprouts, Carrots* (opt) Potato Soup	Lettuce, Spinach, Cucumber & Broccoli Salad *Sprouts, Carrots* (opt) Rye Casserole	Lettuce, Spinach, Cucumber & Broccoli Salad *Sprouts, Carrots* (opt) Barley Casserole	Lettuce, Spinach, Cucumber & Broccoli Salad *Sprouts, Carrots, Peas* (opt) Barley Casserole	Lettuce, Spinach, Cucumber & Broccoli Salad *Sprouts, Carrots* (opt) Barley Casserole	Lettuce, Spinach, Cucumber & Broccoli Salad *Sprouts, Carrots, Peas* (opt) Rye Casserole	Lettuce, Spinach, Cucumber & Broccoli Salad *Sprouts, Carrots* (opt) Barley Casserole
Dinner	Lettuce/Spinach Salad Irish Potato Corn Zucchini Squash	Lettuce/Spinach Salad Irish Potato Beets Green Peas	Lettuce/Spinach Salad Irish Potato Carrots/Celery Cabbage	Lettuce/Spinach Salad Irish Potato Corn Broccoli	Lettuce/Spinach Salad Irish Potato Cauliflower Green Peas	Lettuce/Spinach Salad Irish Potato Yellow Squash Green Beans	Lettuce/Spinach Salad Irish Potato Carrots/Sprouts Baby Limas

*See enlarged options under "Goodies" section

Sample Consuming Schedule A

5:30 am	Arise
5:35 am	Naturalax II, 3 capsules with 8 oz. water
	Acidophilus, 1 capsule
	(Bathe)
6:00 am	Cayenne, 1 tsp. in 4 to 6 oz. water, then chase with more water
	Apple cider vinegar, 1 tbls.
6:10 am	Molasses, 1-1/2 tbls.
6:25 am	Wheat germ oil, 1-1/2 tbls.
	(Depart for work)
7:00 am	Red clover combination, 1 capsule with 8 oz. water
9:00 am	Apples, 2
	Multivitamin, 1
	Kelp, 2 tablets
10:30 am	Almonds, 6 to 12
	Raisins, 1 to 2 tbls.
12:20 pm	Cayenne, 1 tsp. in 4 to 6 oz. water, then chase with more water
	Apple cider vinegar, 1 tbls.

12:30 pm	Raw vegetable salad (lettuce, spinach, broccoli, cucumber, grated carrot, alfalfa sprouts) seasoned with sweet basil, garlic/olive oil/vinegar dressing
	Barley casserole with carrots, peas, onions, green peppers, fresh minced garlic, and seasonings
	Naturalax II, 3 capsules with a little water
2:30 pm	Grape juice, 4 oz., diluted with 4 oz. water
3:30 pm	Pears, 2
5:10 pm	Cayenne, 1 tsp. in 4 to 6 oz. water, then chase with more water
	Apple cider vinegar, 1 tbls.
5:20 pm	Wheat germ oil, 1-1/2 tbls.
5:30 pm	Littlegreen Potato Soup, 1 cup
	Raw lettuce and spinach salad with garlic/olive oil/vinegar dressing, celery seed, cayenne
	Steamed corn with garlic oil and Vege-Sal
	Steamed broccoli with lemon wedge
	Baked potato with garlic oil, chopped steamed green pepper, and Vege-Sal
7:30 pm	Red clover combination, 1 capsule with 8 oz. water
8:30 pm	Molasses, 1-1/2 tbls.
9:30 pm	Naturalax II, 3 capsules with 8 oz.water

Sample Consuming Schedule B

5:55 am	Arise
6:00 am	Naturalax II, 2 capsules with 8 oz.water
	Acidophilus, 1 capsule
6:15 am	Cayenne, 1 tsp. in 4 to 6 oz. water, then chase with more water
	Apple cider vinegar, 1 tbls.
6:25 am	Molasses, 1 tbls.
6:40 am	Raw vegetable juice: 8 oz. carrot, 1 oz. spinach, 1 oz. celery, 1/2 oz. parsley
7:00 am	Blended, slow-cooked wheat berries, 2 cups, with 2 tbls. currants and 2 tsp. honey
	Multivitamin, 1
	Kelp, 2 tablets
	B-12, 1
	Vitamin C, 1 (1000 mg)
	Wheat germ oil, 1 tbls.
	(Bathe)
8:00 am	Red clover combination, 1 capsule with 8 oz. water
	(Depart for work)
9:00 am	Apple, 1
10:00 am	Cashews, 1/4 cup; Almonds, 1/4 cup; Raisins, 1 tbls.; Prunes, 4
11:40 am	Cayenne, 1 tsp. in 4 to 6 oz. water, then chase with more water
	Apple cider vinegar, 1 tbls.
11:50 am	Molasses, 1 tbls.

11:59 am	Wheat germ oil, 1 tbls.
12:00 pm	Raw vegetable salad (lettuce, spinach, broccoli, green peas, cucumber, grated carrot, alfalfa sprouts) seasoned with garlic/olive oil/vinegar dressing, caraway seed, fresh ground black pepper.
	Rye casserole with broccoli stems, carrots, onions, green pepper, garlic, and seasoned with soy sauce and herbs
3:00 pm	Carrot and celery sticks, 2 each
4:30 pm	Banana, 1 or 2
5:30 pm	Cayenne, 1 tsp. in 4 to 6 oz. water, then chase with more water
	Apple cider vinegar, 1 tbls.
	(Return from work)
6:20 pm	Wheat germ oil, 1 tbls.
6:25 pm	Raw lettuce and spinach salad with garlic/olive oil/vinegar dressing, sweet basil, cayenne, and some added apple cider vinegar
	Steamed carrots/celery/mung bean sprouts
	Steamed green peas
	Baked potatoes, 2 medium large, seasoned with tamari sauce, garlic oil, fresh ground black pepper, fresh chopped parsley
8:00 pm	Apple juice, 4 oz., diluted with 4 oz. water
8:30 pm	Molasses, 1 tbls.
9:00 pm	Red clover combination, 1 capsule with 8 oz. water
9:30 pm	Naturalax II, 2 capsules with 8 oz. water

six

"OK's" and "NO-K's" in Food Combining

We have designed a simple Food Combining Chart to help you determine which foods are compatible with each other. You can see how the arrows in the chart join two groupings and indicate whether they make a good or poor combination. As an example, vegetables combine well with proteins, and they combine well with starches. But proteins and starches do not combine well, so are best not eaten at the same meal. The chart also shows that fruits do not mix well with either proteins, starches, or vegetables.

The reason for this is that different foods require different digestive enzymes, and will require various lengths of time to pass through the stomach and intestinal tract. For example, a food that is digested and absorbed very quickly, such as a fruit, will be held back in the stomach and can become fermented if it is eaten at the same time as other slow digesting foods such as milk, meat, fish, starches, and even vegetables.

To avoid improper digestion and fermentation of food in the stomach and intestines, attention must be paid to how we combine our foods as we eat them. As an example, fruits digest the best when eaten alone, that is, only one type of fruit at a time. We could have 2 pears at once, or 2 peaches at once, but after consuming a pear, it is best to wait at least 30 minutes before consuming another type of fruit. The benefit of proper food combining is that it allows us to extract the **maximum nutritive value** from our food, while **minimizing the amount of putrefaction** that takes place in our stomach and intestines.

Although we have learned the value of proper food combining, we have also learned from our experience that as long as we restrict ourselves to healthy, good quality foods, we can modestly stray from some food combining rules without adversely affecting our digestive system. This doesn't mean we feel free to stray from all the food combining rules. Adding fruit to the cereal grain is the only way that we have done so. For example, in the *Starter Diet* section of this book, we suggest adding apples, unsweetened berries, raisins, or currants to the morning cereal grains. Fruit in combination with the grains seems to provide a more palatable transition when *first starting out* on the Transfiguration Diet. Once we began to blend our cereal grains, it made them a more refined food, and we no longer felt the need to add fruit in order to enhance them. Now we enjoy the grain more without fruit, and we know it is better for us.

Even though sprouts are listed in the protein section of the Food Combining Chart, they can also be treated as a vegetable. Cooking mung bean sprouts with steamed vegetables and consuming them with a potato, or adding alfalfa sprouts to a salad that is consumed at the same time as a casserole, is perfectly acceptable.

Another important aspect of proper food combining is to allow adequate spacing between eating foods of different categories. Some general guidelines we follow are:

- Wait at least 30 minutes after fruit or fruit juice before consuming vegetables, protein, starches, or another type of fruit.

- Wait at least 1 hour after vegetables before consuming fruits or fruit juices.

- Wait at least 1-1/2 to 2 hours after grain before consuming vegetables, fruits, starches, or nuts.

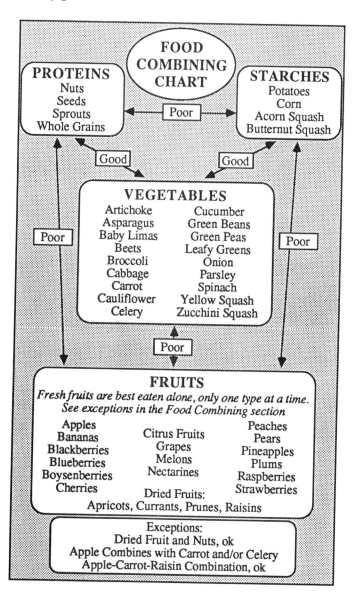

FOOD COMBINING CHART

PROTEINS
Nuts
Seeds
Sprouts
Whole Grains

STARCHES
Potatoes
Corn
Acorn Squash
Butternut Squash

Poor

Good   Good

VEGETABLES

Artichoke	Cucumber
Asparagus	Green Beans
Baby Limas	Green Peas
Beets	Leafy Greens
Broccoli	Onion
Cabbage	Parsley
Carrot	Spinach
Cauliflower	Yellow Squash
Celery	Zucchini Squash

Poor   Poor

Poor

FRUITS
*Fresh fruits are best eaten alone, only one type at a time.
See exceptions in the Food Combining section*

Apples
Bananas
Blackberries
Blueberries
Boysenberries
Cherries

Citrus Fruits
Grapes
Melons
Nectarines

Peaches
Pears
Pineapples
Plums
Raspberries
Strawberries

Dried Fruits:
Apricots, Currants, Prunes, Raisins

Exceptions:
Dried Fruit and Nuts, ok
Apple Combines with Carrot and/or Celery
Apple-Carrot-Raisin Combination, ok

seven

Recipes

Low-Heated Grains

Oat Groats (whole oats)

4	*servings*
2-1/2	*cups whole oats*
	Distilled soak water, to cover the grain, plus 1 inch above the grain
3-1/4	*cups distilled cooking water*
1/4	*teaspoon sea salt*

To Soak: Measure out the grain. Rinse it twice with tap water. Cover the washed grain to 1 inch above the top of the grain with distilled water. Soak for approximately 5 to 6 hours in a cool place (refrigerator) to prevent fermentation.

To Cook: Heat distilled cooking water on the stove to almost boiling (160 to 180 degrees). Pour off the soak water from the grain and put the grain into your warmer-cooker. Add the heated cooking water and sea salt to the grain. This should bring the temperature in the pot to 120 to 130 degrees. Then, cook overnight (8 to 10 hours) on low heat so the temperature of the grain does not rise above 130 degrees. Just turn on the cooker and forget about it until morning. If you prefer more or less juice in the grains, simply adjust the amount of water used during cooking.

Food Warmer-Cooker: This is a restaurant-type food warmer that can maintain a temperature as low as 120 to 130 degrees. You can purchase one at a restaurant equipment supply store, which should be listed in the yellow pages. Eagle and APW are two brands of warmer-cookers that we have used. They come in different sizes, so choose one that is appropriate for the number of people you are cooking for. Also check to be sure that the one you purchase will heat as low as 120 to 130 degrees, since some will not heat below 150 degrees. Usually the actual temperatures are not calibrated on the dial. Most warmer-cookers have either numbered settings or low, medium, and high settings.

To calibrate a new warmer-cooker, fill it part way with water, and, while keeping a candy thermometer in the water, adjust the temperature setting dial until you find which setting results in the water temperature being 125 to 130 degrees. Then place a piece of masking tape above the dial with a pen mark to indicate the right setting. From then on, simply set the dial to the marked setting and it should consistently keep the grain cooking at the proper temperature. It is good to spot check it periodically, however.

Cooking Tips: Until you get a food warmer-cooker, another option is to cook the grain overnight in the oven with just the pilot light on, or by warming the oven to 150 to 180 degrees so that the temperature in the pot remains about 120 to 130 degrees. However, a warmer-cooker is far more desirable, for it is much easier to use than trying to regulate your oven temperature.

For one or two people, whole grains can also be prepared in a thermos. Fill the thermos 1/3 full with whole grain. Add a pinch of sea salt. Fill the remainder of the thermos with boiling water. Seal the thermos, rotate it a time or two so all the grain gets heated evenly, and let it sit overnight. The grain will be ready to consume in the morning. Again, this method isn't as reliable, and you'll find it easier if you eventually get a warmer-cooker.

Soaking and cooking times will vary depending on your location and altitude. You run the least risk of having the grain ferment if you determine the minimum soaking and cooking time that will result in a soft tasty grain. As was mentioned previously, the end product can be unpredictable at times, and you may occasionally discover the grain has fermented and not know why. If you soak it in a cool place (the refrigerator works best), learn how to maintain a temperature of 120 to 130 degrees in your warmer-cooker, and use the minimum soaking and cooking time required, you should have no difficulty. As was said earlier, in the *Starter Diet* chapter, if the cereal grain does ferment during your first trials, you can always have fruit that morning. If the grain for your casserole should ferment, you could easily substitute Littlegreen Potato Soup.

To Serve: In the morning, all you have to do is serve the grain directly from the warmer-cooker into bowls, or you might really enjoy the grain and find it more palatable after it has been blended briefly in a blender. You can add an apple, raisins, currants, or berries (one of these), and honey or maple syrup for sweetener. If you use a blender, you may find the grain more desirable without fruit, maybe with just honey and a sprinkle of cinnamon.

Many individuals have remarked how good the grains are and how the whole grains sustain them for a long period of time. They don't feel hungry so soon after eating as they did on their previous diets.

Wheat Berries

The procedure is the same as for preparing oats, except for the soaking and cooking times. To have the wheat ready by 7 am, start soaking it the day before around 8 am and begin the slow cooking around 7 pm. We also experimented with rye and barley as cereal grains, but found oats and wheat to be the best for us.

Salads

Green Salad

Lettuce

Spinach

Broccoli

Cucumber

Alfalfa Sprouts

Grated Carrot

Green Peas

To Prepare: Use 2 parts lettuce to 1 part spinach. Core and wash the lettuce head. Carefully wash and rinse the spinach leaves. We usually add just a drop of dish soap to the water when washing spinach, then rinse it thoroughly. Cut or tear the lettuce and spinach into bite-sized pieces. Cut washed broccoli buds into small pieces. Cucumbers (preferably unpeeled) can be thin sliced and cut into quarters. Toss all 4 of these ingredients well. Grate some washed, peeled carrots. After serving the salad into bowls, add alfalfa sprouts (1 to 2 tablespoons), grated carrot (enough to give color to the salad), and peas (1 to 2 spoonfuls) per bowl of salad.

Salad Seasonings: You can use garlic/olive oil/vinegar dressing; plain apple cider vinegar; cayenne or fresh ground black pepper; sweet basil; celery seed; caraway seed; fresh chopped parsley; or soy sauce, tamari sauce, or Vege-Sal. Avoid using tamari or soy sauce and Vege-Sal at the same time, to prevent excessive salt intake.

Feel free to use lots of salad dressing on your salad. The salad dressing tastes very good, but you may miss the taste if you don't add an adequate amount. The ingredients in this dressing are nutritious and beneficial to the body, so you need not be concerned about using too much.

Use of Food Processor: When preparing vegetables for salads, steaming, or grain casseroles, we have found that a food processor really streamlines the task if you are preparing for more than a few people. It not only saves time and effort, but the results are so much better than when done by hand. The vegetables are uniformly cut which not only looks nice, but is a feature when steaming vegetables because they will cook more evenly.

We use a Cuisinart DLC-7 Super Pro Food Processor. It has several different sized disc blades and a metal blade. You may prefer to tear the lettuce and spinach by hand or cut them with a knife in order to get pieces that are more bite-sized. The food processor tends to cut the green, leafy vegetables into rather large pieces.

For a quick reference, the following is a list of the Cuisinart blade types and sizes that we use to chop, slice, or grate our vegetables:

Vegetable	Blade Type
Lettuce	8 mm disc blade
Carrots	8 mm disc blade
Broccoli Stems	8 mm disc blade
Yellow Squash	8 mm disc blade
Celery	6 mm disc blade
Cucumber	4 mm disc blade
Green Pepper	metal blade
Garlic Cloves	metal blade
Fresh Parsley	metal blade
Grated Carrot	fine shredding disc blade

Lettuce/Spinach Salad

Lettuce

Spinach Leaves

To Prepare: Use 2 parts lettuce to 1 part spinach. Core and wash the lettuce head. Carefully wash and rinse spinach leaves. Cut or tear the lettuce and spinach into bite-sized pieces. Choose from the same dressings and seasonings as listed under the *Green Salad* section.

Dressings and Condiments

Garlic/Olive Oil/Vinegar Dressing

4-3/4	*cup yield*
4	*cups cold pressed olive oil*
6	*ounces apple cider vinegar or lemon juice*
1	*teaspoon Vege-Sal*
8	*cloves garlic*

To Prepare: Gather ingredients and tools together. Peel garlic cloves. Cut large garlic cloves in half or in large chunks; small cloves can be left whole. Poke holes in the garlic cloves with a fork to allow flavor to be released. To mix, put oil into a container. Add apple cider vinegar or lemon juice, Vege-Sal, and garlic. Shake, and the dressing is ready to serve. More garlic flavor is obtained if the dressing stands for 1 to 2 days before you begin using it. The dressing does not need to be refrigerated. For many of us on this diet, this is the best tasting dressing we ever had, and it tastes even better since we know how good it is for us.

The best olive oil to use is cold pressed. Two brands that we have used are Bertolli and Berio. They can be purchased in a supermarket or a health food store; however, they are expensive in some areas. The least expensive source we have found for olive oil is a produce market or an institutional food supply store.

Garlic Oil

4   *cup yield*

4   *cups olive oil*

10   *cloves garlic*

To Prepare: Gather ingredients and tools together. Put the oil in a container. Peel garlic cloves and cut the large ones in half or in large chunks; small cloves can be left whole. Poke holes in the garlic cloves with a fork to release the flavor. Add the garlic to the oil. Allow the mixture to set 1 to 2 days.

This makes a great tasting flavoring for baked potatoes and steamed vegetables. It gives a nice soup-like consistency to the grain casseroles. We can't imagine this diet without garlic and olive oil, since they play such an important part in just about everything we consume. In fact, we often refer to the diet as the garlic/olive oil diet.

Horseradish and Mustard Sauces

These sauces not only make a tangy addition to such vegetables as cabbage and cauliflower, they are quick and simple to make. Mustard sauce is made from finely ground mustard powder that can be found in a health food store or supermarket. You can buy fresh horseradish root at a health food store and some super-markets. Horseradish is an herb that stimulates the function of the stomach, pancreas, liver, and intestines, in addition to its well-known effects of opening up the sinuses and breaking up mucus congestion. The root preserves best when unpeeled and kept refrigerated, so when preparing horseradish sauce, cut off just the amount of root you estimate you will need.

To Prepare Horseradish Sauce:

1/2   *cup horseradish root, chopped*

1-1/2   *ounces apple cider vinegar*

Enough beet juice to add a brilliant color (optional)

Cut off a section of the horseradish root, enough to yield 1/2 cup. Peel it and chop it into fine pieces with a knife or in a food processor. Put the 1/2 cup chopped horseradish in a blender, add 1-1/2 ounces of apple cider vinegar, and blend until it becomes a fine, smooth pulp. The pulp should be quite moist but not runny. If you have a juicer, you can enhance the appearance of the horseradish by adding enough fresh beet juice to turn it to a brilliant magenta color. Store the prepared horseradish sauce in a covered container in the refrigerator. It should keep about a week.

To Prepare Mustard Sauce:

1/2   *cup mustard powder*

2   *ounces apple cider vinegar*

1   *ounce distilled water*

Combine the water and apple cider vinegar together (making a mixture that is 2 parts vinegar to 1 part water). Slowly add the liquid mixture to 1/4 cup of the mustard powder. Stir until creamy and smooth. Add the last 1/4 cup of mustard and the rest of the liquid. If the end product is a little too thick, prepare and add more vinegar/water mixture.

Steamed Vegetables

The value of steaming vegetables is that it preserves the water soluble vitamins that would otherwise be lost if the vegetables were cooked in water. We recommend steaming vegetables *briefly* on a high-heat setting to prevent destruction of too many enzymes. Never use aluminum pots since the aluminum can be absorbed into the food.

Basic Steaming Instructions

1. Wash the vegetables thoroughly, and remove any bad spots. You can buy a vegetable brush in the household section of most supermarkets. These work great for cleaning the vegetables you don't peel such as potatoes, cucumbers, yellow or zucchini squash, and celery. We have worked hard to develop a consciousness of wanting to protect our bodies from harmful or toxic substances, and we have found it is very important to carefully examine all the foods we consume and remove any unhealthy parts. Also, when washing the vegetables, avoid having them sit in water too long so they don't lose too many of the water soluble vitamins.

2. Put about 1 inch of tap water into a stainless steel pot. Add approximately 1/8 teaspoon sea salt and 1/8 teaspoon Vege-Sal to each cup of water in the bottom of the pot, or use just Vege-Sal as we do when steaming vegetables for the grain casseroles.

3. Place a stainless steel steamer basket in the pot. The water level should be just below the basket so that the vegetables do not sit in the water. You can get a steamer basket at some supermarkets, Pier 1 Imports, or Joske's and other large department stores. They come in different sizes, so be sure to select ones that fit the size cooking pots you use. They cost only a few dollars.

4. Place the cut, sliced, or whole leafy vegetables in the steamer basket with desired seasonings, cover the pot, and bring the water to a boil on a high-heat setting. When the pot reaches a full steaming boil, turn the heat down just enough to maintain the maximum heat possible without losing too much steam; the less steam that escapes, the fewer vitamins will be lost.

5. Steam the vegetables until they are almost to the desired tenderness, then turn off the heat and let the steam finish the cooking. (Cooking time varies with the type and quantity of vegetables prepared, as well as the altitude.) They should be tender but still have some crispness to them when served. The vegetables will retain a brilliant color when not overcooked, but the color will fade and more

nutrients will be destroyed if they are steamed too long. The average cooking time (from the time you turn on the heat until serving time) is 10 to 15 minutes.

6.   After placing the steamed vegetables in a serving dish, pour some of the seasoned cooking water over them. This will add some flavor and keep them from drying out.

7.   When using garlic for seasoning, use approximately 1-1/2 cloves per pound of raw vegetables.

Vegetable Seasonings

After the steamed vegetables are served, you may choose to add additional seasonings such as tamari or soy sauce, garlic oil, apple cider vinegar, Vege-Sal, a lemon wedge, cayenne or fresh ground black pepper, mustard sauce, or horseradish sauce.

For example, we might add garlic oil and soy sauce to green peas; garlic oil and Vege-Sal to corn; apple cider vinegar or lemon wedge to broccoli; mustard sauce to cabbage; or horseradish sauce to cauliflower. These are just a few ideas; you can have fun experimenting yourself.

Preparation of Vegetables

Littlegreen Harvard Beets

For 4 servings, add 1 inch water to a pot; place a steamer basket in the pot; add 3 cups of peeled, sliced beets and 1 teaspoon minced onion. Steam until tender (approximately 10-15 minutes).

To prepare sauce, combine 1/4 cup honey, 1/2 teaspoon salt, 1 tablespoon olive oil. In a separate container, mix 1 tablespoon arrowroot with 1/3 cup apple cider vinegar to prevent lumps from forming. Slowly add this to the honey, salt, oil mixture. Cook over a medium heat, stirring constantly. The sauce won't start to thicken until it almost reaches the boiling point. Continue to cook and stir until it reaches the desired consistency (10-15 minutes).

If the sauce is too thin, add some more arrowroot. To do this, mix the arrowroot with a little of the sauce to dissolve it, then add it to the pot. Place the cooked beets in a serving pot and pour the sauce over them.

Broccoli	Wash by immersing the broccoli heads in water. Cut off half of the longer stalks. (Excess stalks can be sliced and steamed for use in the casserole.) Break up the broccoli head into serving sizes. One option is to serve with a lemon wedge.
Cabbage	Remove any damaged or dirty outer leaves. Wash and cut the cabbage into wedge-shaped pieces. Serve with mustard sauce or horseradish sauce.
Carrots with Celery & Green Pepper	Cut washed, peeled carrots into round, bite-sized pieces. Slice washed celery into 1/4 to 1/2 inch pieces. Wash and dice some green pepper. Sprinkle sweet basil over the vegetables at the start of steaming. For garlic seasoning: peel garlic cloves and chop them finely. Add the garlic to the vegetables at the end of cooking, when the heat is turned off. The garlic flavor is retained better if the garlic is added at the end of cooking.
Carrots with Celery & Sprouts	Cut washed, peeled carrots into round, bite-sized pieces. Slice washed celery into 1/4 to 1/2 inch pieces. Sprinkle sweet basil over the vegetables at the start of cooking. Season with garlic cloves. Add the rinsed sprouts and garlic when the heat is turned off. (Sprouts don't require more than a few minutes of steaming.)

Cauliflower with Green Pepper	Wash by immersing the cauliflower head in water. Break the cauliflower head into sections. Add some diced green pepper. Season with thyme and finely chopped garlic cloves. Sprinkle the thyme over the cauliflower at the start of cooking, but add the garlic when you turn off the heat. Serve with horseradish or mustard sauce.
Corn on the Cob	Husk the corn, remove all silk, cut off the ends, and place the whole ears (or half ears if the whole ears are too large) into the steamer basket. When served, try adding garlic oil and Vege-Sal for flavoring.
Green Beans with Onions & Almonds	Cut off the ends of the green beans. Slice them into halves or thirds, depending on size. Cut the onion(s) into bite-sized wedges (approximately 1 medium onion per 3 lb. of beans). Add finely chopped garlic when the heat is turned off. After placing the cooked green beans and onions in the serving pot, sprinkle them with slivered almonds. Pour some of the cooking water over the vegetables.

Limas & Onions	Place baby lima beans in the steamer basket. If you are using frozen lima beans, allow them to thaw before steaming them. Add onions that are cut into bite-sized wedges (approximately 1 medium onion for 3 lb. limas). Peel the garlic cloves, chop finely, and add to baby limas when the heat is turned off.
Peas	Frozen peas require very little steaming, you are mainly just warming them up. It is best to thaw them before cooking. Season with finely chopped garlic cloves. Add the garlic to the peas when you turn off the heat.
Yellow or Zucchini Squash with Onions & Green Peppers	Slice the washed, unpeeled squash into 1/2 to 3/4 inch slices. If the squash is large, cut the slices into halves or quarters. Cut the onions into wedges (approximately 1 medium onion for 3 lb. of squash). Add some diced green peppers. If preparing yellow squash, sprinkle some dill seed on them. Add some finely chopped garlic when the heat is turned off.

Baked Potatoes

To Prepare: Wash and scrub the potatoes. Cut out any bad spots. Insert a potato spike lengthwise through the center of each potato.

A potato spike is made of stainless steel or aluminum and is shaped like a long nail. You insert it into the center of a potato before baking it. As the metal heats up, it accelerates the cooking process in the center of the potato. It is preferable to use the stainless steel potato spikes if you can locate them. They can be found at most supermarkets.

Bake the potatoes at 400 degrees for approximately 50 minutes. The time will vary with the number and size of the potatoes as well as the altitude.

Remove the potatoes from the oven, remove the spikes, and squeeze the potatoes gently to soften. Cut open the tops (once lengthwise and once sideways to make a cross), and push in the ends so the potatoes open up. Allow them to cool a few minutes before serving.

Baked Potato Seasonings: Lots of garlic oil and some soy sauce or tamari add the best flavor to potatoes. Garlic oil is very good for you, so there's no need to worry about using too much. You can also add fresh chopped parsley or steamed, chopped green pepper; cayenne or fresh ground black pepper; or Vege-Sal. Use either cayenne or black pepper (not both). Also, it would be best to use only one of the salty items (tamari, soy sauce or Vege-Sal). The flavor of a good potato can be lost if masked by too many seasonings.

Littlegreen Potato Soup

10	*cup yield*
6	*cups distilled water*
6	*teaspoons vegetable broth powder*
1-1/4	*teaspoons Vege-Sal*
3/4	*teaspoon cayenne*
1/2	*teaspoon sweet basil*
1-1/2	*tablespoons soy sauce*
4	*potatoes, medium*
2	*cups green peas*
3/4	*pound carrots*
3 to 4	*celery (stalks)*
1	*green pepper*
1/4	*onion, medium*
8 to 9	*cloves garlic*
	Leftover vegetables, whatever is available

To Prepare: Gather ingredients and tools together. Wash and prepare the fresh vegetables. Peel and slice the carrots. Cut celery stalks into 1/4-inch pieces. Dice the onion and green pepper (keep them separate), and finely mince the garlic.

In a pot, place 1 inch of distilled water and 1 tsp. Vege-Sal. Then place a steamer basket in the pot and add the carrots, celery, and onion. Cover and steam until tender. If using fresh potatoes, peel, wash, and dice them. Then steam them separately from the carrots, celery, and onion.

To conserve time and energy, we found that if we are planning to make this soup, it is easier to prepare extra baked potatoes the evening before when we are already baking potatoes for our evening meal. If you have some leftover baked potatoes, peel them, cut them into chunks, and warm them up with the broth (see next paragraph).

To make the broth, add together in a pot the 4 cups of distilled water, vegetable broth powder, all the spices, and soy sauce. Once the broth is mixed, save 1 cup aside to use later for bringing the soup to the right consistency. Heat the broth until it is good and hot, but do not boil. Then add to the broth all the steamed vegetables, potatoes, green peppers, peas, any other leftover vegetables, and garlic (green peppers, peas, and minced garlic are not cooked).

Mix all the ingredients well. To make the soup the consistency we like it, we now blend it briefly in a blender. This results in a soup that is just slightly chunky, that is, you can see little chunks of potato, carrot, celery, and other vegetables, but no whole vegetable pieces. If needed, add more of the broth you put aside to bring the soup to the desired consistency. It should be a fairly thick soup, not watery.

Before serving, heat the soup until it is good and warm, but not so hot that it will burn your mouth. When we reheat the soup at a later time, we find that it generally needs more liquid. You can mix extra broth any time. To make extra broth, mix some distilled water, vegetable broth powder, Vege-Sal, cayenne, sweet basil, and soy sauce in the same proportions as listed in the recipe.

Live Grain Casseroles

Barley Casserole with Carrots and Peas, or Carrots and Broccoli Stems

4	*servings*
2	*cups barley*
	Soak water (1 inch above the grain)
2-1/2	*cups cooking water*
1/4	*teaspoon sea salt*
6	*carrots, medium*
3/4 to 1	*cup peas*
1/2	*onion, medium*
1/2	*green pepper*
2	*cloves garlic*
2	*tablespoons garlic oil*
1	*ounce tamari sauce*
1/2	*teaspoon savory*
3/4	*teaspoon marjoram*
1/2	*teaspoon Vege-Sal*
1/8	*teaspoon cayenne*

For the barley casserole with carrots and broccoli stems, replace the peas with:

    1   cup broccoli stems

and replace the savory and marjoram with:

    2   bay leaves

    3/4   teaspoon sweet basil

    3/4   teaspoon thyme

To Prepare: The grain requires very little attention while cooking, but preparation starts the day before to allow adequate time for soaking and low heating (slow cooking). For example, we start soaking the barley around 3 pm, start cooking it and adding the vegetables and seasonings at 6 to 8 pm. The proportion of grain to vegetables is about 50/50. It is ready by the next morning. You can take some grain casserole with you in a thermos to have for lunch at school or work, or you can let it continue to slow cook until noon if you have your noon meal at home. It may sound like a lot of trouble at first, but once you adjust to a timing strategy, you will realize it isn't difficult at all, and you will agree it is worth it. These grain casseroles are so satisfying, and the herb seasonings make them delicious as well.

Measure out the barley, rinse it twice with tap water, and soak it in distilled water for 3 to 5 hours. While the barley is soaking, keep it in a cool place, preferably the refrigerator, to prevent fermentation.

Wash and prepare the vegetables. Peel and slice the carrots, cut celery into 1/4 to 1/2 inch slices. Thin slice the broccoli stems. Dice the green peppers and mince the garlic. (Refer to "Use of Food Processor" in the *Salad* section.)

Before it is time to start cooking the grain, some of the harder vegetables (carrots, onions, broccoli stems, and celery) will need to be steamed. If using bay leaves, put these in to cook with the steamed vegetables. Peas, green peppers, garlic, and other seasonings go into the casserole without precooking. We usually don't add the peas until morning. If using frozen peas, we thaw them out before adding them to the casserole.

Approximately 12 hours before serving, heat the distilled cooking water to 160 to 180 degrees, or almost boiling. Pour off the soak water from the grain and place the grain into your warmer-cooker. Add the heated distilled water and sea salt to the grain. The temperature of the grain should then be about 110 to 126 degrees.

Add all the vegetables (some of which have been steamed) and seasonings. Cover the warmer-cooker and turn it on to the appropriate heat setting. Let the grain cook on low heat. The temperature inside the warmer-cooker should not rise above 130 degrees if the grain is to remain alive.

Before serving the casserole, check the seasonings and add cayenne, Vege-Sal, or other seasonings to taste.

Rye Casserole with Carrots and Peas

4	servings
2	cups rye
	Soak water (1 inch above the grain)
2	cups cooking water
1/4	teaspoon sea salt
5 to 6	carrots, medium
1	cup peas
1/2	onion, medium
1/2	green pepper
2	cloves garlic
2	tablespoons garlic oil
1	ounce tamari sauce
2	teaspoons fresh chopped parsley
1/2	teaspoon sage
3/4	teaspoon thyme
1/4	teaspoon Vege-Sal
1/8	teaspoon cayenne

Use the same procedure as for preparing barley casserole, except the rye needs more soaking time and a little

more cooking time. To have it ready by, say 7 am, we put it on to soak the day before around 8 am and start cooking it around 7 pm. The times are approximations and can be adjusted to fit in with your schedule.

Wheat berries can also be used for grain casserole. You can experiment with a variety of vegetables and add a great variety of seasonings to the different grains, according to your choice.

eight

Healthy Extras

      To achieve maximum benefit from a proper diet, other health aids also need to become a regular part of our lives. Herbs, exercise, imagery, sunshine, deep breathing, and positive thinking all play important roles in our total well-being, so we want to briefly introduce our thinking regarding these areas.

Herbs

Herbs are natural foods for the vehicle that can assist in regulating the glands, cleansing and rebuilding organs and tissues, and tonifying the vehicle in its weak areas. A cleansing diet alone can gradually clear out accumulated toxins and mucus from the vehicle, but herbs will greatly accelerate the regenerative, rebuilding process. There are specific herbs for every organ and tissue of the body. We believe they were created with the intention that they be used for maintaining the health of the vehicle. To list the herbs and their usages would require a book in itself, so we refer you to the many published sources available to guide you in this area; for example, *School of Natural Healing,* by John R. Christopher; *Natural Healing with Herbs*, by H. Santillo; *The Herb Book*, by John Lust; and *Back to Eden*, by Jethro Kloss.

We want to acknowledge Dr. John R. Christopher, LaDean Griffin, Dr. N. W. Walker, and Paul C. Bragg for their exceptional contribution in the fields of health and nutrition. Their works, both related to herbs and to mucusless diet show us that their material is very advanced both in concept and content.

Following are a few of the herbal remedies we found very helpful as nutritional aids. We present these as an introductory guide to some uses of herbs for those who have no familiarity with

them. This information is not intended for the purpose of prescribing treatments. Many of the following herbal formulas we use are Nature's Way products and can be found in most health food stores, but we do not endorse this brand over any other. In addition, we have included a list of herbs we use in the form of teas for beverages and for supplying nutrients to various organs.

Herbal Formulas

Breathe-Aid: Marshmallow root, mullein, comfrey leaves, lobelia, and chickweed. These herbs promote healing throughout the respiratory tract, and have been helpful for cold or flu symptoms.

Catnip and Fennel extract, fennel seed capsules, or catnip and fennel seed tea: These are valuable for relieving stomach and intestinal gas.

Change-O-Life: Black cohosh, sarsaparilla root, Siberian ginseng, licorice root, false unicorn root, blessed thistle, and squaw vine. These herbs help all the glands to maintain a proper hormonal balance. It is a good nutritive supplement, particularly during puberty and menopause.

Fem-Mend: Golden seal root, blessed thistle, cayenne, uva ursi, crampbark, false unicorn root, red raspberry leaves, squaw vine, and ginger root. This combination can assist in regulating the menstrual cycle, and has been effective for some in relieving cramps or excessive bleeding.

HAS: Brigham tea, marshmallow root, burdock root, golden seal root, chaparral, parsley, cayenne, and lobelia. This formula contains a natural antihistamine and helps decongest the sinuses. It may give relief to symptoms resulting from hay fever, allergies, or sinusitis.

Naturalax II: A lower-bowel tonic containing cascara sagrada bark, barberry bark, cayenne, ginger, golden seal root, lobelia, red raspberry leaves, turkey rhubarb root, and fennel seed. This combination breaks loose old toxic fecal matter in the colon and feeds the peristaltic muscles of the colon so that they will begin to function normally.

Red Clover Combination: Red clover blossoms, chaparral, licorice root, peach bark, Oregon grape root, echinacea, cascara sagrada bark, sarsaparilla root, prickly ash bark, burdock root, and buckthorn bark. This combination is used as a blood purifier. It is an excellent nutritional supplement for anyone with chronic or degenerative disease or for accelerating the cleansing process along with the Transfiguration Diet.

Silent Night: A combination of hops, scullcap, and valerian root. These herbs are food for the nervous

system. They are calming, relaxing, and can promote a restful sleep.

Wild Lettuce and Valerian Extract: These herbs provide nutrients that quiet nerves. The combination is a natural sedative and relieves minor pain.

Drink at least eight ounces of water when taking capsuled herbs. This helps them dissolve better, and prevents any burning in the stomach.

Herb Tea Preparation

To make an **infusion** (a tea made from leaves, flowers or stems): Bring distilled water to a boil. Remove from heat. Add the herbs to the water and steep 10 to 15 minutes. Strain and serve plain or with an optional tsp. of honey.

To make a **decoction** (a tea made from bark or roots): Add herbs to cold distilled water in a pot. Slowly bring the water and herbs to a boil on medium heat. When it reaches boiling, turn down to low heat and simmer 30 minutes. Strain and serve either plain or with an optional tsp. of honey.

Beverage Teas (infusions or decoctions) are usually made with 1 slightly rounded tsp. of the herb to 1 cup of water.

Medicinal Teas can be made much stronger, using as much as 1 to 2 oz. of an herb to 1-1/2 pints of water. One ounce of leafy or flower herbs is about one handful.

Some Commonly Used Herbs

Black Walnut: Contains organic iodine that is antiseptic and healing; a powerful vermicide (kills worms); reduces fever; rich in potassium, magnesium, and silica (food for nails, skin, and nerve sheaths); a blood purifier.

Used For: Skin diseases; relaxed or ballooned intestines; any bleeding surfaces; tumors; cancers; sore throat; tonsillitis; dandruff; a valuable gargle.

Burdock Root: One of the best blood-purifying agents for chronic infection and skin diseases; relieves congestion of lymphatics; increases flow of urine; is healing to all of the urinary tract; promotes elimination through the skin.

Used For: All skin diseases (pimples and boils, eczema, psoriasis, rashes, cancer); kidney and urinary deposits; congested lymphatics.

Camomile: Improves appetite; aids digestion by improving blood flow to stomach lining; increases flow of blood to skin surface which will produce sweating; kills worms; very soothing to the nerves; a good hair rinse; mild pain reliever; a general tonic.

Used For: Indigestion, weak stomach, ulcers; headache; nervousness; neuralgia; colds and fevers; bronchitis.

Catnip: Relaxant; nervine; sedative; anti-flatulent; pain reliever; antacid.

Used For: Flatulence; colic; griping (intestinal cramps); spasms; restlessness; nervous headache; mild pain relief.

Comfrey: Soothing and healing to all mucus membranes in respiratory and digestive tract; a cell proliferant (promotes growth of cells); astringent; nutritive; expectorant; blood cleanser; styptic (stops local bleeding by constricting blood vessels). It promotes the growth of new bone and new flesh; stops hemorrhage; heals inflamed tissues. One of the finest healers for the respiratory system.

Used For: Cough; inflamed lung conditions; bronchitis; asthma; hemorrhage of the lungs; pneumonia; inflamed stomach or bowels; fractures; bruises; sprains; open sores or wounds; anemia; sinusitis; burns; insect bites.

Echinacea: A blood and lymph purifier; a powerful antiseptic, anti-putrefactive agent; anti-venomous.

Used For: Septic or putrefactive conditions; congested lymph; snake bites; healing tissue wherever there is decay or when there is pus, gangrene, blood poisoning; enlarged prostate gland; bleeding gums; abscesses; sores; cancer.

Fennel: Used for treating gas; acid stomach; colic and cramps. In strong doses, will remove obstructions of liver, gall bladder, and spleen.

Hops: Relaxing nerve tonic; produces soothing sleep in nervous conditions; dissolves urinary stones; increases flow of bile and tones liver; relieves mild pain; stomach tonic; mild blood cleanser.

Used For: Sleeplessness; nervous conditions; indigestion; liver problems; neuralgia.

Horseradish: Promotes stomach secretions and digestion; excellent for sinus congestion and urine retention. Stimulates function of the pancreas.

Used For: Sinus trouble; sluggish liver and stomach; stomach and intestinal catarrh; indigestion; neuralgia; poor circulation; bronchitis. Start with 1/4 tsp. grated horseradish root, moistened with apple cider vinegar. Hold it in your mouth until it is nothing but sawdust (the fragrance is gone). It will immediately start cutting the mucus loose. You can work up to 1 tsp. 3 times a day. (Fresh root is much stronger than dried.)

Mullein: Soothing and healing to all mucous membrane linings, but has a special affinity for the respiratory organs; anti-asthmatic; anti-catarrhal; an herbal pain killer with narcotic properties; calming and quieting to inflamed and irritated nerves; promotes expectoration from lungs; eases cough; antiseptic; germicide; kills worms.

Used For: Pain; all lung diseases, cough, asthma, hay fever, bronchitis; nasal congestion or catarrh; tonsillitis; sore throat; ulcers; sinusitis; swollen joints; inflammatory rheumatism.

Peppermint: Anti-nausea; aids digestion; a stimulant that quickly diffuses through the system and brings back to the body its natural warmth in case of sudden fainting, dizzy spells, extreme coldness or pale countenance; a cleanser for the entire body; reduces fever; promotes perspiration (in strong doses); a soothing sedative; anti-flatulent; strengthens nerve and heart muscles; anti-spasmodic.

Used For: Nausea, dizziness, coldness, stomach and intestinal gas, nervous headache, restlessness, sleeplessness, neuralgia, spasms of stomach or bowel, fevers, fainting, flu (in combination with elder flowers), and it is good when used as a beverage tea.

Red Raspberry: Blood purifier; astringent; tonic; stimulant; stomach tonic; anti-nausea; antiseptic; antacid; antispasmodic.

Used For: Blood cleansing; removing cankers in the mucous membranes of the mouth; nausea; gas and indigestion; colds; fevers; flu; sore mouth; spongy gums; ulcers and wounds; female menstrual problems. It is rich in iron. Drink copious amounts hot during colds or flu.

Scullcap: The best nervine in nature; antispasmodic; calmative for restlessness, tremors, and hypersensitivity; tones and soothes the nervous system.

Used For: Nervous headache; hypersensitivity; insomnia; nervous exhaustion; neuralgia; aches and pains; convalescence from fevers.

White Willow Bark: Pain killer; reduces fever and chills; antiseptic; a stomach tonic; relieves heartburn; anti-nausea.

Used For: Headaches, body aches; neuralgia; fevers; painful joints; infected wounds; gargle for sore throat; canker sores (apply powder directly to mouth sore).

Wood Betony: Nervine; digestive tonic; kills worms; opens obstructions of liver and spleen; remedy for head and face pains. Combines well with scullcap.

Used For: Pains of the face and head; neuralgia; indigestion; jaundice; biliousness; heartburn; stomach cramps; colic pains; colds, flu, worms, and poisonous snake bites.

Combination Herb Teas

Burdock Root, Echinacea Root, & Black Walnut: 2 parts burdock root, 1 part echinacea, 1 part black walnut. Mix 2 tsp. of the combination per cup of water.

Comfrey Leaf & Mullein: 2 parts comfrey to 1 part mullein. Mix 1-1/2 tsp. of the combination to 1 cup water.

Fennel & Catnip: 1 tsp. of bruised (slightly crushed) fennel seeds and 1 tsp. catnip per cup of water.

Peppermint & Camomile: 1 rounded tsp. peppermint per cup of water with 1/2 tsp. camomile flowers.

Scullcap, Hops, & Wood Betony: 2 parts scullcap, 1 part wood betony, 1 part hops. Mix 2 tsp. of the combination per cup of water.

Exercise

The goal is to find some form of exercise suitable to you that will stimulate circulation, improve the function of the heart, and increase lung capacity. Brisk walking, swinging arms by your side, is about the best exercise that anyone can do. If you can find time to spend about 30 minutes walking in the sun and doing some deep breathing, this can be very beneficial to your overall health.

Jogging is good, but requires more caution; it is not suitable for everyone. Swimming is an excellent exercise that works out every part of your body, and is very helpful for anyone with arthritis, back pain, or any muscle and joint disorders. Home exercising equipment such as rowing machines, stationary bicycles, and treadmills have proved very valuable and convenient. A mini-trampoline for running in place is a good home exercising tool also. We may be different from some in that we don't recommend exercising for muscle building or body shaping. To us, the value of exercise is that it tonifies the vehicle and promotes healthier circulation and breathing.

Reflexology/Acupressure

Reflexology is a technique of massaging certain reflex areas on your feet and hands. These reflex areas on the soles of the feet and palms of the hands are connected to various organs, nerves, and glands in the body. The reflexology massage can send a surge of stimulation or activity to the areas that need help, in order to increase vitality, relieve pain, clean out congestion, heal chronic illnesses, or build resistance to disease. You can do this massage yourself at any time.

Acupressure or contact healing is a do-it-yourself technique of pressing with your fingertips on acupuncture points in the body. It is a technique to create a smooth flow of energy throughout the body by contacting various points on energy "meridians" or pathways, which relate to various organs, glands, and tissues. If the organ, gland, or area the point represents is not functioning well, the point will be sore, indicating an energy leak at that point. Applying pressure to that area restores the normal energy flow.

We have used acupressure and reflexology as needed for various minor ailments, and have achieved very good results.

Imagery

Mental imagery can be used by any individual as a method of healing or rebuilding or correcting weak areas in the human vehicle. If your vehicle has difficulty with chronic constipation, for example, you can mentally *visualize* the peristaltic action of the colon working and moving the contents of the colon along. If someone's vehicle has difficulty walking due to arthritis, it is possible that he can improve by mentally *imaging* himself walking with ease.

One imagery tool you can use that we all have found very helpful is a "shower mantra." During the shower you can say to yourself, "I'm washing away all negativity and disease. They are flowing out of my body, going down the drain. My body feels happy, healthy, pure, and positive." (Then imagine the drain drawing out all the negativity.) It works.

Positive Thinking

To receive maximum benefit from the diet and healing aids we mention, they must be accompanied by positive thinking. In the same way, to be effective in applying the principles of genetic reprogramming, we have to learn to refuse to see any situation as a negative. We've grown to know that out of every seeming difficulty we encounter, there is potential for positive growth, if we choose to reach up in our thinking to see the situation from a higher perspective.

It works for us to remember that the mind and vehicle are separate, and that we (the minds) only want improvement and we know only positive thoughts. Anything less than this comes from the vehicle (the voice of genetic programming from the ancestral heritage and/or environment).

In other words, the mind doesn't feel discouragement, guilt, fear, defensiveness, or think, "No one likes me" or "I can't do anything right." If we have the thought, "I feel so depressed," then we have to gain some objectivity and recognize it's the vehicle talking. One way to respond is to say, "Vehicle, I am not depressed. I'm not going to listen to that. I am happy. I want to spend my energy in better ways."

If forty times a day we say to ourselves, "There's no way I can quit smoking," then how can we do otherwise? Instead of making a strong stamp on a negative thought, why not turn it around by consciously repeating to the vehicle many times a day, "I can quit smoking. I want to be healthy and have clear lungs. It's easy to quit."

Our minds *are* stronger than our vehicles. If we (the minds) exert a strong voice, we can override the genetic impulses of the vehicle, and the vehicle also can become happy, healthy, and positive. From our experience, we've learned that the vehicle *can* change its old ways, and by expecting it to, we make it happen.

Where Our Team Is Going

Littlegreen, Inc.'s Think Tank is an organization dedicated to continuing exploration of radically advanced concepts geared toward achieving not only a purer, toxin-free body, but also a toxin-free mind.

Physical and mental disciplines are often compromised in order to make them easier and more palatable to the general public. However, we are focusing on the special segment of individuals who want to go "all the way"--those who have tired of the diluted approaches to diet and behavioral disciplines and have come to know "there's got to be something more."

We are not only dedicated to the pursuit of a physical diet that surpasses all other diets aimed at a disease-free body, but we are also dedicated to the pursuit of a mental diet that surpasses all other disciplines aimed at a disease-free mind--one that rises above destructive concepts and toxin causing behavior.

Your Possible Involvement

Various ways that you can stay abreast of our Think Tank's findings, and take advantage of our efforts are detailed on the last page of this book.

List of Specialty Items and Where to Get What

ITEM	SOME AVAILABLE BRANDS or TYPES	AVAILABLE AT:
Food Processor	Cuisinart	Department Stores
Food Warmer-Cooker	Eagle, APW	Restaurant equipment supply
Juicer	Acme, Champion	Health food store
Potato Spikes	Stainless steel, preferably	Supermarket
Steamer Baskets	Vita-Saver, Pier I	Supermarket, Pier I Department stores
Apple Cider Vinegar	Heinz	Health food store, Supermarket
Blackstrap Molasses	Plantation	Health food store
Cayenne	Pure cayenne only	Health food store
Cold Pressed Olive Oil	Berio, Bertolli	Health food store, Supermarket, Produce market
Distilled Water	-----	Health food store, Supermarket
Kelp Tablets	Schiff	Health food store
Vegetable Broth Powder	Dr. Jensen's Broth or Seasoning	Health food store
Wheat Germ Oil	Viobin	Health food store
Whole Grains: Hard Red Winter Wheat Oat Groats Pearled Barley Whole Grain Rye	Arrowhead Mills	Health food store, Supermarket (If stores in your local area do not carry whole grains, ask the store managers to order them for you)
Acidophilus	KAL, Biogenics	Health food store
Bulk Herbs	Seasoning & Medicinal Herbs	Health food store, Herb shop (Seasoning herbs are cheaper when purchased in bulk rather than in bottles)
Herbal Preparations (capsules, extracts & ointments)	Nature's Way, Nature's Herbs, Nature's Plus, Nature's Sunshine	Health food store, Herb shop
Multivitamin/Mineral Supplement	Twin Lab (Daily One Caps), Nu-Life, Schiff, KAL	Health food store
Naturalax II	Nature's Way	Health food store
Red Clover Combination	Nature's Way	Health food store

Bibliography

1. Carter, Mildred. *Helping Yourself with Foot Reflexology*. Parker Publishing Company, Inc., West Nyack, New York, 1969.

2. Christopher, Dr. John R. *Capsicum*. Research and compilation by Lotus Bailey. Christopher Publications, Springville, Utah, 1980.

3. Christopher, Dr. John R., M.H. *Dr. Christopher Talks on Rejuvenation Through Elimination*. Dr. Christopher, Provo, Utah, 1976.

4. Christopher, Dr. John R., M.H. *Dr. Christopher's Three-Day Cleansing Program, Mucusless Diet and Herbal Combinations*. Dr. Christopher, Springville, Utah, Revised Edition, 1978.

5. Christopher, Dr. John R. *School of Natural Healing*. BiWorld Publishers, Inc., Provo, Utah, 1976.

6. Ehret, Prof. Arnold. *Prof. Arnold Ehret's Mucusless-Diet Healing System*. Ehret Literature Publishing Co., Inc., Dobbs Ferry, New York, 20th Edition, 1983.

7. Gray, Robert. *The Colon Health Handbook*. Emerald Publishing, Reno, Nevada, 10th Revised Edition, 1985.

8. Griffin, LaDean. *Is Any Sick Among You.* BiWorld Publishers, Provo, Utah, 1974.

9. Houston, F. M., D.C. *The Healing Benefits of Acupressure: Acupuncture Without Needles.* Foreword by Linda Clark. Keats Publishing, Inc., New Canaan, Connecticut, 1974.

10. King, Serge. *Imagineering for Health.* The Theosophical Publishing House, Wheaton, Illinois, 1981.

11. Kirschner, H. E., M.D. *Live Food Juices.* H. E. Kirschner Publications, Monrovia, California, 1957.

12. Kloss, Jethro. *Back to Eden.* Back to Eden Books, Loma Linda, California, 1985.

13. Lust, John, N.D., D.B.M. *The Herb Book.* Bantum Books, Inc., New York, New York, 1974.

14. Null, Gary and Staff. *Food Combining Handbook.* Jove Publications, Inc., New York, New York, 1973.

15. Nutrition Search, Inc., John D. Kirshmann, Director, Lavon J. Dunne, Co-author. *Nutrition Almanac.* McGraw-Hill Book Company, 2nd Edition, 1984.

16. Pearson, Durk and Shaw, Sandy. *Life Extension: A Practical Scientific Approach*. Warner Books, Inc., New York, New York, 1982.

17. Santillo, Humbart, B.S., M.H. *Natural Healing with Herbs*. Edited by Subhuti Dharmananda, Ph.D. Hohm Press, Prescott Valley, Arizona, 1984.

18. Scott, Cyril. *Cider Vinegar: Nature's Great Health-Promoter*. Athene Publishing Co., Ltd., Wellingborough, Northamptonshire, England, 1981, Eighth Edition, 1982.

19. Walker, Norman W., D.Sc., Ph.D. *Colon Health: The Key to a Vibrant Life*. O'Sullivan Woodside & Company, Phoenix, Arizona, 1979.

20. Walker, N. W., D.Sc. *Fresh Vegetable and Fruit Juices: What's Missing in Your Body?* Compiled under the direction of and endorsed by R. D. Pope, M.D. O'Sullivan Woodside & Company, Phoenix, Arizona, 1936, Revised 1978.

21. Wigmore, Ann. *Be Your Own Doctor*. Avery Publishing Group, Wayne, New Jersey, 1982.

22. Wigmore, Ann. *Hippocrates Live Food Program*. Hippocrates Press, Boston, Massachusetts, 1984.

Index

Christopher Publications

Additional Titles By Dr. John R. Christopher

DR. CHRISTOPHER'S HERBAL SEMINAR VIDEOS (8 VHS tapes) Now available to the public! Over 16 hours of Dr. Christopher on VHS video cassette. Witness America's premier natural healer sharing his knowledge and philosophies gained through years of experience. #99100 • $395.00

SCHOOL OF NATURAL HEALING *Revised Edition* This monumental work groups herbs by therapeutic actrion, and treats in great detail their usage and actrion. A majority of the 1,000's of herbal formulas used by Dr. Christopher can be found in this book. Also discussed are diseasess, their symptoms and causes, and case histories. This new edition contains Dr. Christopher biography, expanded index, improved format, updated research. #99101 • $39.95

DR. CHRISTOPHER'S NEW HERB LECTURES (10 cassette tapes - 1 hour each) Listen and glean from the knowledge, wit and wisdom of Dr. Christopher teaching the benefits of herbs and natural healing. Special mind trac summaries at the end of each tape will aid the student to retain this vital information. #99102 • $69.95 (set includes 2 bonus tapes)

EVERY WOMAN'S HERBAL The wisdom of Dr. Christopher combined with the practicality of Cathy Gileadi for the health of women of all ages. 242 pages. #99110 • $14.95

HERBAL HOME HEALTH CARE This volume from Dr. Christopher effectively deals with over 50 common ailments, listing the diseases in convenient alphabetical order with concise definitions, symptom descriptions, causes, herbal aids and other natural treatments. 196 pages. #99103 • $12.95

CAPSICUM Dr. Christopher's research and case histories detailing the uses and healing powers of cayenne pepper. 166 pages. #99109 • $6.95

JUST WHAT IS THE WORD OF WISDOM? Learn how the Word of Wisdom prompted Dr. Christopher toward a higher way of healthy living. #99105 • $2.00

DR. CHRISTOPHER'S THREE DAY CLEANSE, MUCUS-LESS DIET AND HERBAL COMBINATIONS Juice cleansing for detoxification, wholesome diet for health. #99106 • $2.00 • *Also in Spanish #99104S • $2.00*

THE COLD SHEET TREATMENT Dr. Christopher explains step by step his time tested treatment for colds, flu and any feverous or viral condition. #99107 • $2.00

THE INCURABLES Treatment program for conditions deemed "incurable". Dr. Christopher shows "there are no incurable diseases". #99108 • $2.00

AN HERBAL LEGACY OF COURAGE The first biography of Dr. Christopher. Learn about his youth, his roots in herbalism, and his joys and struggles as he sought to heal and educate all who would hear. #99112 • $5.00

DR. MOM by Sandra Ellis. One mother's discovery of the power of herbs opens the way for her to heal many afflictions that come upon her family. Gain wonderful knowledge from this firsthand account. #99509 • $7.95

Call or write to:
Christopher Publications
P.O. Box 412 • Springville, UT 84663
1–800–372–8255